HUDSON'S ENGLISH HISTORY

A COMPENDIUM

ROGER HUDSON

WEIDENFELD & NICOLSON

First published in Great Britain in 2005
by Weidenfeld & Nicolson
10 9 8 7 6 5 4 3 2 1

Compilation and contemporary text © Roger Hudson 2005
Design and layout © Weidenfeld & Nicolson 2005

A CIP catalogue record for this book is available
from the British Library.

ISBN 0 297 84415 6

Design director: David Rowley
Designed by Nick Robertson
Picture research by Annabel Merullo

Printed and bound in Great Britain

Weidenfeld & Nicolson
The Orion Publishing Group Ltd
Wellington House
125 Strand
London, WC2R 0BB

I have some idea of writing my son a child's History of England,
to the end he may have tender-hearted notions of War and Murder,
and may not fix his affections on wrong heroes, or see the bright
side of Glory's Sword and know nothing of the rusty one.
Charles Dickens to Angela Burdett-Coutts, 1843

A country that ignores its past has no future.
Niccolo Machiavelli

TABLE OF CONTENTS

—————————— THE VICTORIAN AGE ——————————

MEDIEVAL ENGLAND

THE KNIGHTS OF THE ROUND TABLE

Arthur and his knights may be the stuff of legend rather than history, denizens of mythical Albion alongside Hereward the Wake, Herne the Hunter and Robin Hood, but at English royal funerals a statue was sometimes carried, painted with his arms, three gold crowns on an azure ground. Richard I rode out of Vézelay with a sword which purported to be Arthur's Excalibur, when on the Third Crusade, though later in Sicily he exchanged it for four transport ships and fifteen galleys. When Edward III founded the Order of the Garter in 1344 it was modelled on the chivalric fellowship of Arthur's knights, while Henry VII christened his eldest son Arthur. Even in Victorian England their doings were considered suitable subjects for the frescoes painted by William Dyce in the Queen's Robing Room in the New Houses of Parliament, next to the Gallery where Daniel Maclise painted Nelson at Trafalgar and Wellington at Waterloo.

In Chapters 10 and 11 of Book XIX of Sir Thomas Malory's *Le Morte Darthur* (completed 1470), the tale is told of Sir Urre of the Mount, 'a good knight in the land of Hungary' who arrived at King Arthur's court, 'at that time was holden at Carlisle'. Sir Urre had been wounded seven times when slaying another knight, whose mother, a witch, had put a spell on the wounds so that they would not heal 'until the best knight of the world had searched his wounds.' King Arthur arranged for all at court to 'handle' him. 'At that time there were but an hundred and ten of the Round Table, for forty knights were that time away [including Sir Lancelot]... When it is full complete, there is an hundred knights and fifty.' The episode provides Malory with a splendid excuse to catalogue the resonant names of those who were there – in fact numbering rather fewer than 110.

THE KINGS, DUKES AND EARLS

KING Clarance of Northumberland
SIR Barant le Apres, that was called the King with the Hundred Knights
KING Uriens of the land of Gore
KING Anguish of Ireland
KING Nentres of Garloth
KING Carados of Scotland

DUKE Galahad, the haut prince
Constantine that was Sir Carados' son, of Cornwall, that was KING after Arthur's days
DUKE Chaleins of Clarance
THE EARL Ulbause
THE EARL Lambaile
THE EARL Aristause

THE NOBLE KNIGHTS OF THE ROUND TABLE

SIR Gawaine with his three sons, Sir Gingalin, Sir Florence and Sir Lovel
SIR Agravaine
SIR Gaheris

SIR Mordred
SIR Gareth, that was of very knighthood worth all the brethren

SIR LAUNCELOT'S KIN:

SIR Lionel
SIR Ector de Maris
SIR Bors de Ganis
SIR Blamor de Ganis
SIR Bleoberis de Ganis
SIR Gahalantine
SIR Galihodin
SIR Menaduke
SIR Villiars the Valiant
SIR Hebes le Renoumes

SIR Sagramore le Desirous
SIR Dodinas le Savage
SIR Dinadan
SIR Bruin le Noire, that Sir Kay
named La Cote Male Taile
SIR Kay le Seneschal
SIR Kay de Stranges
SIR Meliot de Logris
SIR Petipas of Winchelsea
SIR Galleron of Galway
SIR Melion of the Mountain
SIR Cardok
SIR Uwaine les Avoutres
SIR Ozanna le Cure Hardy
SIR Astamor
SIR Gromere, Grummor's son
SIR Crosselm
SIR Servause le Breuse, that was
called a passing strong knight ... had
never courage nor lust to do battle
against no man, but if it were against
giants, and against dragons, and wild
beasts
SIR Aglovale
SIR Durnore
SIR Tor, that was begotten upon
Aries, the cowherd's wife [King
Pellinore begat these last three, as
he did] Sir Lamorak, the most
noblest knight that ever was in
Arthur's days as for a worldly knight,
traitorously slain by Sir Gawaine and

his brethren, and Sir Percivale that
was peerless except Sir Galahad in
holy deeds, but they died in the
quest for the Sangrael
SIR Griflet le Fise de Dieu
SIR Lucan the Butler
SIR Bedivere his brother
SIR Brandiles
SIR Clegis
SIR Sadok
SIR Dinas le Seneschal of Cornwall
SIR Fergus
SIR Driant
SIR Lambegus
SIR Clarrus of Cleremont
SIR Cloddrus
SIR Hectimere
SIR Edward of Carnarvon
SIR Priamus that was christened by
SIR Tristram the noble knight, and
these three were brethren
SIR Helaine le Blank
SIR Brian de Listinoise
Three brethren that Sir Launcelot
won upon a bridge in Sir Kay's arms:
SIR Gautere, SIR Reynold, SIR
Gillemere
SIR Guyart le Petite
SIR Bellangere le Beuse, son to the
good knight Sir Alisander le
Orphelin that was slain by the
treason of King Mark. Also that
traitor king slew the noble knight Sir
Tristram, as he sat harping afore his
lady La Beale Isoud, with a trenchant
glaive [sharp sword] . . . La Beale
Isoud died swooning upon the corse
of Sir Tristram, whereof was great
pity
SIR Hebes
SIR Morganore
SIR Sentraile
SIR Suppinabilis
SIR Bellangere le Orgulous, that the

good knight Sir Lamorak won in plain battle

SIR Nerovens and SIR Plenorius, two good knights that Sir Launcelot won

SIR Darras

SIR Harry le Fise Lake

SIR Erminide, brother to King Hermaunce, for whom Sir Palomedes fought at the Red City with two brethren

SIR Selises of the Dolorous Tower

SIR Edward of Orkney

SIR Ironside, that was called the noble Knight of the Red Launds, that SIR Gareth won for the love of Dame Liones

SIR Arrok de Grevaunt

SIR Degrane Saunce Velany that fought with the giant of the black lowe [hill]

SIR Epinogris, that was the king's son of Northumberland

SIR Pelleas that loved the lady Ettard, and he had died for her love had not been one of the ladies of the lake, her name was Dame Nimue, and she wedded Sir Pelleas, and she saved him that he was never slain

SIR Lamiel of Cardiff that was a great lover

SIR Plaine de Fors

SIR Melleaus de Lile

SIR Bohart le Cure Hardy that was King Arthur's son

SIR Mador de la Porte

SIR Colgrevance

SIR Hervise de la Forest Savage

SIR Marrok, the good knight that was betrayed with his wife, for she made him seven year a were wolf

SIR Persaunt

SIR Pertilope, his brother, that was called the Green Knight

SIR Perimones, brother to them both, that was called the Red Knight, that Sir Gareth won when he was called Beaumains

'All these hundred knights and ten searched Sir Urre's wounds by commandment of King Arthur.' Chapter 12 then tells how Sir Launcelot returned at the right moment and 'was commanded by Arthur to handle his wounds, and anon he was all whole, and how they thanked God ... And even Sir Launcelot wept as he had been a child that had been beaten.'

HUNTSMEN AND HOUNDS OF THE ROYAL HOUSEHOLD, *c.* 1136

Hornblowers .... four at 3d a day
Serjeants .... twenty at 1d a day
Fewterers (keepers of greyhounds) .... 3d a day each
and 2d for their men
and for each greyhound .... a halfpenny a day
The King's pack of hounds .... 8d a day (does this imply
there were eight couple?)
Knight-huntsman .... 8d a day
Huntsmen .... 5d a day each
Leader of the lime-hound
(leashed and only loosed to kill a stag at bay)
and the lime-hound .... a halfpenny a day
Berner (feeder of hounds) .... 3d a day
Huntsmen of the hounds on the leash .... 3d a day each
Of the great leash .... four hounds at 1d a day
Of the small leashes .... six should have 1d
For the great leash .... two men, 1d a day each
For the small leashes .... two men, 1d a day each
Brach keepers (small hounds hunting by scent) .... 3d a day each
Wolf hunters, ... 20d a day for horses,
men and hounds, and they should have
twenty-four running hounds and eight greyhounds,
and £6 a year to buy horses – but they say £8
Archers who carry the King's bow .... 5d a day each
Bernard, Ralf the Rober, and their fellows .... 3d a day

MONKS, FRIARS AND CANONS

BENEDICTINES (called black monks from the colour of their habits, O.S.B. – Order of St Benedict) the oldest monastic order, founded by St Benedict in the sixth century at Monte Cassino in Italy. His Rule, only some 12,000 words long, established the pattern of communal living, chastity, the absence of personal possessions, of obedience to the abbot, and the form of worship. As well as a long night-office, there were seven day offices: Matins or Lauds (daybreak), Prime (6 a.m.), Terce (9 a.m.), Sext (noon), Nones (3 p.m.), Vespers (sundown) and Compline (9 p.m.). The humanity of St Benedict is seen in his provision that the first psalm of the night-office be said slowly to give lie-abeds time to make it into church. Each week all the psalms were read, and each year, most of the Bible.

The monasteries (and nunneries) were founded and endowed by the nobility to serve as strongholds to defend them from the dangers abroad in the supernatural world, as powerhouses of prayer and fasting which could discharge on their behalf any penances imposed upon them, and as places where younger sons and daughters could spend their lives in a manner fitted to their station. As a consequence of these functions, there was a tendency towards elaboration in every aspect of the Benedictine life, and especially in worship. In the early centuries Benedictine monasteries were independent of each other but, after its foundation in 904, the one at Cluny in Burgundy became the mother house to a great family of affiliated CLUNIAC monasteries. By 1135 there were 24 in England alone.

This organisation in some respects served as a model for the CISTERCIANS (white monks) one of the new orders that started to emerge at the end of the eleventh century, looking to cut away the accretions that had gathered round the original Benedictine idea, simplify the very lengthy Cluniac liturgy and rediscover a deeper and more personal religion. They did not rely on endowments such as churches, tithes, rents and services and instead located themselves in apparently barren lands on the frontiers of the then civilised world. Here they farmed aggressively, using illiterate lay brothers to do the manual labour, and built huge but unadorned abbeys such as Fountains, Rievaulx and Tintern. By avoiding embellishment and elaboration, surpluses were created, especially from the sale of wool, and these were spent on acquiring more land. By the death, in 1153, of St Bernard of Clairvaux, the force behind the Cistercian expansion, there were more than 400 Cistercian houses.

The AUGUSTINIAN CANONS (also known as Austin or black canons, O.S.A. – Order of St Augustine) were the other type of new order, priests deriving their rule from a single letter of St Augustine about the problems of leading a communal life: holding all things in common, praying together, dressing without distinction, obeying a superior. Many different groups evolved under this vague and elastic umbrella, and most of the foundations were modest ones, located near towns or castles and much involved in everyday life, running schools, hospitals and looking after the elderly.

Shortly after 1100 two military orders emerged in the Holy Land, recently captured as a result of the First Crusade: the KNIGHTS HOSPITALLER and the KNIGHTS TEMPLAR. They took vows of poverty, chastity and obedience and their task was to protect the Holy Places and the pilgrims going to them. It was much easier to fulfil a vow to go on crusade by making an endowment to either of these orders than to set out for Palestine oneself, so they soon became wealthy.

In the thirteenth century the growing importance of towns and of the new universities like Paris, Bologna and Oxford called forth a new monastic variant: the mendicant (begging) friars. The two most significant orders were the

DOMINICANS (black friars, O.P. – Order of Preachers) and the FRANCISCANS (grey friars, O.F.M. – Order of Friars Minor). They were an attempt to reach out into the new centres of population, and to practise a simpler religious life according to the precepts of Christ. St Dominic's initial aim was to combat the Albigensian heresy, based on the belief that the flesh was evil, in Languedoc. His weapon was the pulpit and he soon concentrated his efforts on the universities where preachers could be recruited and trained. Students were happy to enrol because it meant they could abandon the scramble for ecclesiastical preferment. St Francis was much less focused initially, except in the literalness with which he and his followers took the vow of poverty. But very soon the two orders were copying each other, the Franciscans' adopting Dominican organisation and also turning towards the universities, while the Dominicans adopted the Franciscans' attitude to poverty, which ensured them a good reception in towns. Both needed concentrations of people in order to beg successfully since their rules precluded holding income-generating property. By 1300 there were some 80,000 friars roaming throughout Christendom.

The CARTHUSIANS were founded by St Bruno at the same time as the Cistercians. Henry II founded the first English Charterhouse at Witham in Somerset as part of the penance imposed on him after the killing of Thomas à Becket, and St Hugh of Lincoln came from the mother house of La Grande Chartreuse to put it on its feet, but their great period in England began in the second half of the fourteenth century, with seven new Charterhouses founded by 1420. Theirs was an attempt to combine the rigours of the hermit's existence with a measure of communal life. They abstained from meat, ate one meal a day, wore hair shirts, kept unbroken silence, lived in separate cells with separate gardens where they grew their food, and only worshipped together for some services.

--- OTHER ORDERS ---

ARROUAISIANS Augustinian Canons who led a more contemplative life.

AUSTIN FRIARS Began as congregations of hermits and then under the Rule of St Augustine from 1256.

BONSHOMMES These followers of the Augustinian Rule had a house at Ashridge in Herts and, much later, at Edington in Wilts.

BRIDGETTINES Founded by Bridget of Sweden c. 1350. Nuns with resident monks as spiritual advisers.Henry V founded a Bridgettine convent at Syon on the banks of the Thames.

CARMELITES Founded in the Holy Land as the Order of Our Lady of Mount Carmel and later reconstituted as friars (white friars).

CRUTCHED FRIARS Also known as Friars of the Cross. Arrived in

England in 1244, followed the Rule of St Augustine and worked chiefly in hospitals.

FRIARS OF THE SACK Offshoots of the Friars Minor, though much more given to study than to the roving life of ordinary friars. Arrived in England in 1257, the order was abolished in 1274, which meant no new members could be recruited. It lingered on into the 14th century.

FONTEVRALDINES Founded by itinerant preacher Robert d'Arbrissel at Fontrevault in the Loire valley in 1100, double order of monks and nuns under an abbess.

GILBERTINES The only order originating in England, at Sempringham in Lincolnshire in *c.* 1131. Founded by St Gilbert as a double order of nuns and canons under the rule of St Augustine, though many later houses were only for canons. Gwenllian, daughter of Llwelyn, the last Prince of Wales, was sent to Sempringham in 1283 by Edward I after he conquered Wales. Here she died in 1337, the last Princess of Wales.

GRANDMONTINES Founded by Stephen of Muret (d. 1124), a particularly austere order.

OBSERVANTS Reformed Franciscans advocating a return to a purer version of their founder's rule, from later fourteenth century on.

PREMONSTRATENSIANS (white canons) Founded at Premontre by St Norbert in 1120 and following a strict version of the Rule of St Augustine.

TIRONESIANS Founded at Tiron in early twelfth century and influenced by the Cistercians.

TRINITARIANS Also called Maturins or Red Friars, though not mendicants. Their particular task was to ransom Christian captives of the Saracens, in the last resort by offering themselves as substitutes for the captives. Their houses were centres for collecting funds and for recruitment. They ran some hospitals too. Miguel de Cervantes, author of *Don Quixote,* was ransomed by them in 1580, five years after his capture by the Barbary corsairs of Algiers.

VICTORINES Augustinian canons of St Victor in Paris, noted for scholarship and mysticism.

—— THE NAMES OF THE BELLS OF CROWLAND ABBEY ——

(a Benedictine monastery in the Lincolnshire fens)

Bega, Pega, Turketyl, Tatwin, Beltyn, Bartholomew, Guthlac

BRATTICES, MANGONELS AND TORTOISES: A SIEGE GLOSSARY

As castles evolved and their defences were strengthened, increasing ingenuity was applied to the devices and techniques used in sieges. Ideas for the more advanced siege engines came back with the returning crusaders from the East, where the Byzantine Empire had continued to use ones based on the classical Roman models.

ALLURE Wall walk with no protection on the inside so that if besiegers reached it, they could be shot at from the rest of the castle.

ARBALEST Crossbow.

BALLISTA Large siege engine which, working on the bow principle, fired javelins with considerable accuracy.

BARBICAN Strongly fortified towered castle gatehouse.

BATTERING RAM Tree or large baulk of timber hung from a wheeled framework by chains so it could be swung against the base of a wall. Protected above by a penthouse.

BELFREY Tower moved on wheels or rollers, several stories high, with a drawbridge at the top, used for attacking castle walls. Variant names for it: Beffroi, Berfror, Berefredium, Malvoisin. The largest such tower recorded was the one Richard I had constructed before Acre in 1191, called Mategriffin – checkmate.

BORE Heavy pole with sharp iron head for penetrating walls. Called mouse, cat or sow.

BRATTICE Wooden gallery built out from parapets to enable attackers immediately below to be shot at through slots in the floor.

BRICOLE Stone-throwing siege engine.

CASEMATE Gallery outside base of a castle's curtain wall for defence against miners, battering rams, etc.

CRENELLATION see Merlon.

CROW Hook on end of long arm for pulling down defences or catching attackers.

EMBRASURE see Merlon.

GYNOURS Men in charge of siege engines.

HOARDING see Brattice.

LOOP Slit in wall to fire arrow or cannon from.

MACHICOLATION Brattice built from stone.

MALVOISIN (literally 'bad neighbour') see Belfrey.

MANGONEL Siege engine consisting of vertical beam between two uprights with cords twisted between them. Beam then pulled back by winch, with a stone loaded onto its end, before being released. Torsion of cords produced propelling power. Stone described an elliptical flight so could go over a wall and fall inside fortifications.

MANTLET Angled timber or wicker shield on wheels.

MERLON Stone part of crenellations on top of a castle wall between embrasures.

MINE Defences were undermined and then the pit props holding up the tunnel were set on fire. Such mines were often countermined by the defenders.

MOULON see Mangonel.

MURDER HOLE (also called Meutrieres) Slot in ceiling of gatehouse passage through which attackers could be killed. One of the objects or substances dropped down was red-hot sand, which could penetrate the chinks in armour.

ONAGER Siege engine.

PAVISE (also Pavas) Large portable shield.

PENTHOUSE Wooden roof to protect miners.

PETRARIA (also Petrary or Perrier) Mangonel or stone-throwing engine.

PORTCULLIS Grating or grille in doorway that retracted into the space above.

POSTERN Small gate at side or rear of a castle.

SCORPION see Petraria.

SPRINGAL (or Espringal) see Ballista.

TORTOISE Penthouse or mantlet protecting men working a battering ram.

TREBUCHET Stone slinging machine worked by counterpoise – a lever on a fulcrum with heavy weights suspended from forward end of lever. The other end of the lever holding the stone was hauled down using a windlass and then released. In 1339 the French used one to launch dead horses into the castle at Thin, and in 1345 a captured messenger was launched back into Auberoche. In 1346 the Tartar army besieging the Genoese at Caffa in the Crimea on the Black Sea became infected with the Black Death. They used a trebuchet to sling corpses into Caffa and so spread the disease. The Genoese abandoned Caffa and sailed back into the Mediterranean, taking the Black Death with them, thus spreading it throughout Europe.

PLACES OF PILGRIMAGE IN MEDIEVAL ENGLAND

BAWBURGH, near Norwich	St Walstan, an 11th-century peasant
BEVERLEY	St John, died 721, founder of Beverley Abbey
BURY ST EDMUNDS	St Edmund, King of the East Angles, shot to death by the Danes, 869
CANTERBURY	St Thomas à Becket, Archbishop, murdered 1170
CHESTER	St Werbergh (Werburga), died 699, nun and daughter of the King of Mercia
CHICHESTER	St Richard, Bishop, died 1253
DURHAM	St Cuthbert, died 687, Bishop of Hexham and Lindisfarne
ELY	St Etheldreda, died 679, daughter of King of the East Angles
EVESHAM	Simon de Montfort, killed in battle 1265. Leader of the opposition to King Henry III. Never canonised and in fact twice excommunicated
FINCHALE	Godric, died 1170, a much-travelled merchant who became a hermit here, three miles NE of Durham; never canonised
GLASTONBURY	The supposed tombs of King Arthur and Queen Guinevere were discovered here at the end of the 12th century and the Abbey claimed to have the Holy Grail, the cup used by Christ at the Last Supper. It was an object of quest for King Arthur's knights and was meant to have been brought to England by Joseph of Arimathea, from whose staff the Glastonbury Thorn was meant to have sprung
GLOUCESTER	Edward II, King of England, murdered 1327. Never canonised
HAILES ABBEY	Gloucestershire. The blood of Christ

HEREFORD	St Thomas Cantilupe, Bishop, died 1282
IPSWICH	The Virgin Mary's milk
LEICESTER	Thorn from the Crown of Thorns at Church of St Mary's in the Newarke
LINCOLN	St Hugh, Bishop, died 1200
LONDON	St Erkenwald, Bishop, died 693, at St Paul's Cathedral
	St Edward the Confessor, King of England, died 1066. Christ's footprint left on a rock at his Ascension into Heaven. Blood of Christ given by the masters of the Knights Templars and Hospitallers of Jerusalem to Henry III in 1247 – all at Westminster Abbey
NORTH MARSTON, Bucks	Master John Shorne, 13th-century priest of the parish, never canonised. At one point his remains were taken to St George's Windsor, but they were not efficacious there so were taken back to North Marston
NORWICH	St William, a boy apprentice supposedly ritually murdered by the Jews in 1144. (Little St Hugh was a similar supposed 'child-saint' victim of the Jews, venerated at Lincoln. The 9-year-old boy died in 1255 and 18 Jews were hanged for the crime.)
OXFORD	St Frideswide, an Anglo-Saxon princess-nun, died *c.* 735
ROCHESTER	William of Perth, a simple pilgrim murdered nearby when on the way to Rome
ST ALBANS	St Alban, died 303. England's first Christian martyr. Crown of Thorns. St Amphibalus. Supposed fellow-martyr of St Alban, arising from a misunderstanding of the Latin word for a priest's cloak
SALISBURY	St Osmund, Bishop, died 1099
WALSINGHAM, Norfolk	Miraculous statue of the Virgin Mary, and some of her milk
WALTHAM	Miraculous Cross of black marble found in the reign of King Cnut

WINCHESTER	St Swithun, Bishop, died 862
WINDSOR	Henry VI, King of England, died 1471. Never canonised
WORCESTER	St Wulfstan, Bishop, died 1095
YORK	St William, Archbishop, died 1154

As this list indicates, for the medieval pilgrim in search of a cure for his bodily ills, or doing penance for his sins, there were many local alternatives to the great shrines of St Thomas at Canterbury or Our Lady of Walsingham. Many of the saints here are bishops attracting pilgrims – and income – to the cathedrals in their dioceses. There were several other 13th-century bishops, besides St Richard of Chichester and St Thomas Cantilupe of Hereford, who enjoyed popular cults after their deaths, but who were never canonised: Roger Niger of London, Robert Grosseteste of Lincoln, Walter Suffield of Norwich, James Berkeley of Exeter and William March of Wells. When a papal commission met in 1307 to decide whether Thomas Cantilupe should be made a saint, one of the main testimonials to his posthumous miracle-working powers came from William ap Rhys, also known as William Cragh (the scabby), who had been hanged three times on the same day in 1290, yet lived to tell the tale. The first time the rope broke, the second time the gallows collapsed and, when being laid out for burial after the third apparently successful execution, he started to move again. He claimed that, on the way to the gallows, he had invoked the recently dead Thomas Cantilupe, while Mary de Briouze, wife of the English Lord of Gower who had ordered the execution, said she had prayed to the same Thomas to restore life to the criminal's corpse. The authorities decided that since the bishop had intervened to save William's life, he should be let off. The fabric of several cathedrals and abbeys benefited from the offerings and fees generated by the shrines within them. The non-existent St Amphibalus helped pay for the west front of St Albans, St Thomas for the enlargement of Hereford's nave and Edward II for much building at Gloucester Abbey. The Church authorities tried to discourage a number of local cults; for instance, that of Simon de Montfort at Evesham ended after 1300. From the later 14th century on the policy was to encourage devotions centred on the Virgin Mary and on Christ, but pilgrimages remained very much part of popular religion right up to the Reformation. The catalogue of places he has visited at home and abroad, recited by a palmer (pilgrim) in a play written in the 1530s by John Heywood, testifies to this:

> At Saynt Toncomber and Saynt Tronion,
> At Saynt Bothulph and Saynt Anne of Buckston,
> On the hylles of Armony, where I see Noes ark.
> With holy Job, and St George in Suthwarke,
> At Waltham and at Walsyngham,

And at the good Rood of Dagnam,
At Saynt Cornelys, at Saynt James in Gales,
And at Saynt Wynefrydes well in Walles,
At Our Lady of Boston, at Saynt Edmundes Byry
And Streyght to Saynt Patrick's purgatory.
At Rydeboe and at the blood of Hayles,
Where pylgrymes paynes ryght muche avayles,
At Saynt Davys; and at Saynt Denis,
At Saynt Matthew and Saynt Marke in Venis'
At mayster Johan Shorne, at Canterbury,
The great God of Katewade, at Kynge Henry,
At Saynt Savyours, at our lady of Southwell,
At Crome, at Wylsdome and at Muswell,
At Saynt Richarde and Saynt Roke,
And at Our Lady that standeth in the oke.
To these with other many one
Devoutly have I prayed and gone,
Prayeng to them to pray for me
Unto the blessed Trynyte.

Toncomber = St Uncumber or Wigefortis, who grew a beard and a moustache because she did not wish to marry and as result was crucified by her irate father, the King of Portugal

Armony = Armenia
Gales = Galicia (Compostella)

THE LONGBOW AND THE CROSSBOW

The bow dates back to prehistory and, indeed, arrowheads 50,000 years old have been found. Crossbows dating from the 3rd century BC survive in China. Roman cavalry were equipped with SHORTBOWS or COMPOSITE BOWS made from wood, horn and sinew. Horn was glued to the belly side (facing the archer) of the wooden core of the bow, and sinew to the other side. When the bow was released the horn expanded while the elastic sinew contracted. This made the speed of return to the normal position greater than with an all-wooden bow and so the arrow travelled faster. However, in the Dark Ages the secret of the composite bow seems to have been forgotten in the West, which allowed the wooden long bow to have its finest hour.

On the visual evidence of the Bayeux Tapestry, both short conventional bows and longbows were used at the Battle of HASTINGS, and it is known that the Normans also had crossbows there. King Harold of England died of an arrow in the eye at the battle. William Rufus was killed by an arrow while out hunting in 1100. In the century that followed, the crossbow became dominant throughout Europe and on the Crusades. Richard I was wounded in the knee by a crossbow bolt in 1196 at a siege in Brittany and finally killed by a bolt while besieging the castle of Chaluz in France in 1199; in fact, one originally fired by his own men then retrieved and reused by the enemy. The disadvantage of the crossbow was its slow rate of fire and its limited range of 200 yards. Its advantage was that it required less strength and skill to use than a longbow.

Methods of SPANNING (cocking, or drawing the string of) the CROSSBOW evolved down the years:

✠ By placing one's feet against the bow either side of the stock (or tiller) and then pushing the feet away whilst holding the bowstring until it engaged with the trigger.

✠ Placing a foot in a STIRRUP attached to the end of the stock, with the leg bent. The leg was then straightened, allowing the archer to engage the bowstring, which he was holding, with the trigger mechanism.

✠ A CLAW device was attached to a belt round the archer's waist by a short cord. The claw was hooked round the bowstring while the archer bent forward; he then straightened his back, so bringing the string to the trigger mechanism.

✠ Instead of a claw a PULLEY with a hook was used, and the hook was put round the bowstring. The cord going round the grooved rim of the pulley was attached to the stock at one end and to the archer's waist at the other. Again, the archer straightened his back. (This can be clearly seen in Antonio and Piero Pollaiuolo's painting of the *Martyrdom of St Sebastian* in the National Gallery.)

✠ A GOAT'S FOOT LEVER (so-called from its shape, in French a pied-de-biche, a hind's foot) with a claw at one end which fixed under the string; the lever pivoted on a pin going through the stock when pressure was applied to its other end, so drawing the bowstring back.

✠ The STEEL BOW developed during the 15th century, greatly increasing the range of the crossbow up to 390 yards; but since it had a pull of 1500 lbs it normally necessitated the use of a full-blown WINDLASS with pulleys, wound by handles on either side, to pull back the bowstring.

✠ The final development was the CRANEQUIN or RACK, which had a metal ratchet bar and a winder with meshing cogs. It was a very slow method because the handle had to be turned about thirty times, taking thirty-five seconds as opposed to twelve with a windlass. For this reason it was mostly used for hunting.

✠ A BACKSIGHT could be fitted to a crossbow, in the form of a notched strip of wood. The archer's right thumb fitted into one of these notches and he then looked along line between thumb and top of the head of the bolt.

Using a Cranequin

Towards the end of the 13th century Edward I seems to have realised the potential of the LONG BOW during his campaigns, first in Wales and then in Scotland. Many of his archers were from Gwent (South Wales) or from the forests of Nottinghamshire and Derbyshire, or from Cheshire. The best bows were of seasoned yew and care was taken to have heartwood on the belly side and sapwood on the other, which gave some of the same benefits as the composite bow. Those found in the sunken wreck of the Tudor warship the *Mary Rose* confirm just how big long bows were, ranging from over six feet to just under seven. Archers would have had to be at least five feet, seven inches tall. Arrows found with draw-lengths of between 28 and 30 inches confirm these dimensions. These bows were of between 80 and 160 pounds draw-weight, and had a range of up to 300 yards. The strength and training required to use them effectively was considerable. The simultaneous pulling back of the string, using three fingers, and pushing forward of the bow was done from a lowered arm position, the bow then being raised to the full draw position before being released. The positioning of the archer's trunk in relation to the drawn bow explains why the expression 'shooting in a long bow' is used.

The English learnt from the Scots that formations of well positioned infantry were more than a match for heavy cavalry, but they also learnt at the battle of FALKIRK in 1298 how vulnerable to volleys of English arrows the tightly packed schiltrons or squares of Scottish spearmen were. At DUPPLIN MOOR in 1332 and HALIDON HILL in 1333 they combined these two lessons, using dismounted men-at-arms flanked by archers, who could inflict big casualties on the advancing Scots before they could get to grips with the infantry. England, as compared with France, suffered from a chronic shortage of heavy cavalry. In the early 14th century there were probably only 3,000 English capable of fighting as knights, because of the great expense involved. Later Edward III never had more than 5,000, which was only one-sixth of what France could bring into the field at the height of the Hundred Years' War. So sheer necessity also drove the English towards what turned out to be the winning tactical combination.

Although the archers proved their worth first against the French at the naval battle of SLUYS in 1340, then at MORLAIX in 1342, it is the part they played at CRECY in 1346 that is remembered. The Crecy campaign began with the taking of Caen, where 105 Normans were killed when they foolishly exposed their backsides to the English archers. At Crecy itself the French cavalry charged at least 14 times but on each occasion were met by a rain of arrows. An archer could loose off ten arrows a minute, so in theory 3,000 could loose off 60,000 in two minutes. The mercenary Genoese crossbowmen fighting for the French were meant to soften up the English at the start of the battle but were simply swept aside (they had been ineffective at Morlaix too). The few primitive guns which the English had must have been about as useless, except perhaps for their psychological impact. The allowance of arrows per man at Crecy was 100, but even so the archers took every opportunity during lulls in the fighting to go forward to retrieve arrows from the ground or from corpses. The fighting went on into the night, by moonlight, and only ceased at midnight.

At POITIERS ten years later the French attacked largely on foot, but this did not prevent their defeat, with the English archers playing the greatest part in it. The only problem, it seemed, was to maintain the levels of training and skill among the class from which English archers were recruited. For instance, in 1369 Edward III ordered the sheriffs of London to forbid any sports that might distract men from practising archery, including football, handball, throwing of stones, and cock fighting. Such a stern approach may or may not have been instrumental in the final great victory owed to the long bow in France at AGINCOURT in 1415. Half the English archers were in fact mounted in this campaign, though of course dismounting to fight. Henry V called them his 'yew hedge', and told them to equip themselves with sharpened stakes which they could drive into the ground and then retreat behind if attacked by cavalry – a standard tactic from here on. Henry's culminating exhortation to his men is recorded as, 'Fellas let's go.' At the end of the battle there were 10,000 French dead, including half the nobility

of France, while English casualties were a few hundred at most. The French accused the English of poisoning their arrows because so few survived arrow wounds. A more likely explanation is that wounds festered because the arrow tips were rusty. The effect of arrow wounds on horses was certainly often devastating, driving the animals frantic as each movement they made increased the pain. Before the battle the French had threatened that they would cut off the fingers of any archers they captured. Afterwards the English taunted their enemy by brandishing their fingers in the V sign. At the battle of VERNEUIL in 1424 there were many Scottish archers on the French side but they were outshot by the English, and another massacre approaching the scale of Agincourt followed. Thereafter the French learnt their lesson and employed well-trained archers of their own in large numbers. Free companies of archers were created, levied by parish, one man for every 80 hearths. By Louis XI's reign there were 16,000.

It was the growing use of handguns that brought an end to the dominance of the long bow. When the French defeated the English at CASTILLON in 1453, there were 700 handgunners in the French ranks. Henry VII had 2,000 French mercenaries armed with handguns when he wrested the throne from Richard III at BOSWORTH in 1485, though the opinion is that they were not a vital ingredient in his victory. In the first year of Henry VIII's reign 40,000 yew longbow staves were bought from Venice, but the defeat of the Scottish army at FLODDEN in 1513 is pointed to as the last battle where the long bow was decisive, and by the end of the sixteenth century it was obsolescent.

'Suppose I was in that wood yonder, and had in my hand a bow of the red yew, ready braced, with a strong taut string, a straight, round arrow shaft with a well shaped nock, with long low fletchings bound with green silk, and a sharp-edged steel head, heavy and strong, of green-blue temper, that would draw blood out of a weather cock; suppose I had my foot on a tussock, my back to an oak tree, the wind at my back, the sun to my side, and the girl I love best, close by, to watch me. I would shoot such a shot, so strong and deep drawn, so sharply loosed, so low in flight, that it would be no better for my enemy if he wore a breastplate and a Milan hauberk than a wisp of fern, a kiln rug, or a herring net.'
– *Iolo Goch, bard to Owain Glyndwr, leader of the last Welsh rising against the English in the early 15th century*

PLAGUE AND DISEASE

LEPROSY The most conspicuous disease of the earlier Middle Ages was in fact a number of different skin complaints. The first leprosarium to isolate sufferers was set up in Spain in 1067 by El Cid. By the thirteenth century there were over 19,000 leprosaria throughout Christendom. In the following century, after the arrival of the Black Death, leprosy seems to have gone into retreat. Two possible reasons are advanced for this, the first to do with an increase in the amount of tuberculosis. Immunity reactions to that overlap with those provoked by the main type of leprosy, so more suffering from tuberculosis meant fewer falling victim to leprosy. The second is to do with yaws, another skin disease put under the general heading of leprosy at the time. Yaws is transmitted by skin-to-skin contact, of which there is presumed to have been less after the Black Death since reduced numbers of people meant there was much more cloth and more firewood to go round, and so less need to huddle together in bed for warmth in the increasingly cold winters of the Little Ice Age which had begun about 1300.

BLACK DEATH or plague. It is generally agreed that there have been three pandemics of the plague: the first in the sixth and seventh centuries AD, the second beginning with the Black Death of 1346–50, and the third which began in China in 1892, reaching India in 1896, where it eventually killed 12.5 million people. The Black Death was brought from an area on the Yunnan/Burmese border, where it was endemic, to the Eurasian steppes by the movements of Mongol hordes. Carried by fleas which in turn can be carried by rats, it was shipped by Genoese traders from the Black Sea into the Mediterranean (see p. 15). It then spread across Europe, arriving at Weymouth in June 1348. The European population may have been more susceptible than earlier because the pressure of population on resources was bringing malnutrition, with less food being produced as marginal lands became exhausted and as the weather got colder. It is very difficult to arrive at an accurate estimate of what the population of England was in 1348, and how many were subsequently killed by the Black Death, but most accept a population of between 3.7 million and 4.6 million with about one-third of them falling victim (1.4 million). It was an agonizing death involving boils in armpits and groin, and neither physical precautions and treatment nor spiritual preventatives such as penance, fasting and the sacrament were of any use. The over-population and under-employment prevalent before meant that recovery after 1350 was surprisingly fast. But the plague struck again catastrophically in 1361 and there were other lesser outbreaks in 1371, 1375, 1390 and into the fifteenth century, particularly in the towns. By 1400 wages had gone up, there was much greater mobility of labour, and more and more services had been commuted for cash payments by landowners as the manorial system broke down. The plague's impact on the Church was also far-reaching. The monasteries never recovered from the death of perhaps half the monks and friars and a hundred of their abbots. The career opportunities outside their walls were now much improved, while incomes were impaired. Much building may have gone on but the Church's authority was never the same, as people increasingly looked for a more personal form of religion.

TYPHUS first appeared in 1490 among Spanish troops in Granada who had previously been in Cyprus. Transmitted to humans by lice, it has always been the particular scourge of armies, causing havoc during the various Italian campaigns of the sixteenth century and during the Thirty Years' War in the seventeenth century. It had plenty of victims during the English Civil War and there were other bad outbreaks in England and Ireland in the first decades of the nineteenth century, in 1837 and 1843, but it is best remembered here under the guise of gaol fever, killing many more than the hangman ever did. The louse was identified as the villain of the piece in 1912 and thanks to this typhus was kept out of the trenches on the Western Front during the First World War by regular delousing of the men and their uniforms.

SYPHILIS also first appeared in an army, a French one outside Naples in 1494–5. There is much controversy over its origin – whether an import from the New World or a mutation of a disease already long-established in Europe

THE ENGLISH SWEATS or sweating sickness, as its name implies, always appears to have begun in this country, first breaking out in 1485 and then recurring at intervals until 1551. It killed within two or three hours of striking its victims. Its exact nature remains a mystery.

THE PLAGUE the Black Death by another name, remained endemic in England throughout the sixteenth and seventeenth centuries. There were particularly bad outbreaks in 1593 (10,000 deaths in London), 1603 (34,000), 1625 (35,000) and 1636–7 (15,000) until the final outbreak in 1665 (100,000). Thereafter it left North-West Europe.

MALARIA was also on the retreat in this part of the world. Increased numbers of cattle as a result of farming improvements provided the blood-sucking anopheles mosquitoes which carry the malarial plasmodium with a good alternative source of food to humans. However, the plasmodium doesn't find cattle a suitable host, so cannot reproduce and spread. The other effect of more cattle was more protein in the diet, which meant more antibodies to deal with all sorts of human infections.

SMALLPOX had, by the seventeenth century, replaced the plague as the principal cause of death. Inoculation – by taking matter from a smallpox pustule and inserting it under the skin of a healthy person – was introduced to England in 1717, and promoted by Lady Mary Wortley Montagu, the wife of the British

Ambassador to Turkey, who had seen it performed in Constantinople and inoculated her own children. Vaccination, using matter from cows suffering from cowpox and therefore safer, was introduced by Edward Jenner, a Gloucestershire doctor, in 1798. He had observed that milkmaids who had suffered cowpox appeared to be immune to smallpox.

YELLOW FEVER another mosquito-borne disease, may have been confined to the tropics but it killed and incapacitated more British soldiers in the West Indies during the Napoleonic Wars than were lost in all the campaigns in the Peninsula: 40,000 killed and a similar number incapacitated. The French lost 33,000 men in Santo Domingo (Haiti) in 1802. (In the Crimean War nearly four times as many British troops died from disease as were killed by the Russians; in the Boer War there were still five times as many killed by disease as by the Boers.)

CHOLERA first appeared in one of the Anglo-Indian armies engaged in the Third Mahratta War in 1817. The troops spread it through northern India and it soon made its way out of the subcontinent. However, it did not reach England until 1831 when some German sailors from Hamburg jumped ship in Sunderland, bringing it with them. The insanitary conditions of the new industrial cities, with inadequate sewers and water supplies, were ideal for the water-borne bacillus, greatly helped to travel round the world by improved steam transport. It produced diarrhoea, vomiting, dehydration, and death, in short order. Medical opinion thought it was transmitted by a miasma in the air, but in spite of this misconception there were moves afoot to improve sanitation in the towns. It struck again in 1848 and then again in 1854. A London doctor, John Snow, mapped deaths from it in the Soho district and realised they clustered round a public water pump in Broad Street. Its handle was removed, and the number of deaths decreased dramatically. In spite of this, it was decades before the miasma theory was supplanted by the germ theory.

TUBERCULOSIS, CHOLERA, DIPHTHERIA, TYPHOID The bacilli of these found in 1882, 1883, 1883, and 1896 respectively. A vaccine against tuberculosis was produced in 1921, methods of guarding against cholera became self-evident once its cause was pinned down, an antitoxin for diphtheria was introduced in 1891, mass inoculations against typhoid started in the 1900s.

INFLUENZA The great influenza epidemic of 1918–1919 killed more people than died in the First World War – between 20 and 50 million worldwide, and 675,000 in the USA alone. Perhaps a majority of the world's human inhabitants fell ill from it. Most victims died because of secondary bacterial invaders proliferating in throats and lungs made vulnerable by the primary influenza attack. There are current concerns about bird flu because experts suspect that the 1918 virus originated in birds before mutating into a human flu virus.

Although the casualty figures for 1918–1919 are shocking, it must be remembered that the Black Death killed a far larger proportion of populations.

'This pestilence [the Black Death] was so contagious that those who touched the dead or the sick were immediately infected and died, so that the penitent and confessor were carried together to the grave . . . Many died of boils, abscesses and pustules which erupted on the legs and in the armpits. Others died in a frenzy, brought on by the affliction of the head, or vomiting blood . . . I, seeing these many ills, and that the whole world is encompassed by evil, wait among the dead for death to come. I leave parchment for continuing the work, in case anyone should still be alive in the future and any son of Adam can escape this pestilence and continue the work thus begun.'

John Clynn, a Franciscan Friar in Ireland, c.1349

DR JOHN SNOW'S MAP OF CHOLERA OUTBREAKS IN SOHO, 1854

- Cholera death
- Water Pump

THE EXCHEQUER, TALLIES AND ROLLS

The original Exchequer was both a piece of furniture and a calculating or computing device, a simple two-dimensional abacus. It was probably introduced to England c. 1100, possibly by Robert Losinga, Bishop of Hereford as well as a distinguished mathematician and astrologer. A table measuring ten feet by five feet, it was covered with a cloth on which lines were ruled, dividing it into squares and so giving it the appearance of a chess board (scaccarium is the Latin for chess). Counters were placed in the squares in such a way as to indicate thousands, hundreds, twenties, ones. One row of squares could be used to display an amount due to the king and that below it the amount actually received from the sheriff of a county. The difference between the two could be seen at a glance by the king's officers and the sheriffs when the latter appeared for the annual audit at Michaelmas (29 September) each year.

THE EXCHEQUER TABLE

	£1,000	£100	£20	£1
Sum due £1,443	•	• • • •	• •	• • •
Sum Received £1,282	•	• •	• • • •	• •

Before the days of Arabic numerals, and the so-called 'pen reckoning' that went with them, this device, using multiples of ten and allowing for a nought by leaving a square blank, was of great service.

Once the calculations had been done and seen to be done on the table-top, they had to be preserved, as a record and as a receipt. The receipt took the form of a TALLY. A piece of wood had name, date and purpose of payment written on it, and was notched with a knife, the notches standing for sums of money. It was then split down its length, the notches remaining visible on both halves. One half of the tally was kept by the treasury and the other was the sheriff's receipt. Though they sound primitive, tallies, like the Exchequer, made accounts three-dimensional and tangible. They were easy to store and very difficult to counterfeit. In any dispute it was simply necessary to see whether the two halves of the tally matched up. They went on being used into the 19th century and in 1834, after the Receipt of the Exchequer had been abolished, a fire made of recent ones spread to the old Houses of Parliament and burnt them down.

The PIPE ROLLS were sheets of parchment on which the treasury scribes recorded accounts in greater detail. The earliest pipe roll dates from 1130. They were so called because they look like lengths of pipe when rolled up. Exchequer parchment was made of sheepskin because it was cheaper and showed up any erasures made on it. (Paper only started appearing early in the 14th century.) England was peculiar in keeping its records in the form of rolls (*rotuli*) rather than books. EXCHEQUER ROLLS were made of two membranes only, stitched together, and less than two metres long. These were then piled on top of each other and held together at the tops by cords. CHANCERY ROLLS were made of several membranes joined by stitching so as to make a continuous length.

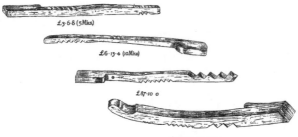

£3·6·8 (5Mks)

£6·13·4 (10Mks)

£87·10·0

£166·13·4 (250Mks)

13th-century Exchequer tallies

CRIMES IN LONDON PUNISHED BY THE PILLORY, 1419

JUDGMENT OF PILLORY FOR :

• Pretending to be a Sheriff's Serjeant, meeting the bakers of Stratforde, and placing them under arrest until they had paid a fine
• Putrid meat
• Forestalment (buying up improperly for a profit) of poultry
• Selling two stinking capons
• A stinking rabbit sold
• Selling a putrid pigeon
• Judgment of imprisonment upon a person for a year and a day, and of pillory each quarter for three hours, with a whetstone tied round his neck, for lies which were disproved
• Pretending to be a Summoner of the Archbishop, and summoning the Prioress of Clerkenwell; as also for pretending to be a Purveyor for the King
• Selling a peck of stinking eels

- Enhancing the price of corn
- Selling oats, good on the outside and the rest bad
- Making false deeds
- Deficiency of coal in sacks
- Rings and buckles made of latten (brass) plated with gold and silver, and sold for gold and silver
- Judgment of the pillory upon certain bakers, who had holes in their tables, called moldyngbordes, by means whereof they stole their neighbours' dough
- Cutting a certain purse
- Taking away a child, to go begging with him
- False dice, with which he played and deceived people
- A false obligation (forged bond)
- A certain false and counterfeit letter
- For a deception committed, namely, counters (jettons or Nuremberg tokens made of brass) passed as gold
- Lies uttered against the Mayor and Aldermen
- Selling a stinking partridge
- Lies uttered against William Walworthe (former Mayor and the slayer of Wat Tyler, who had died in 1385)
- Begging under false pretences
- Soothsaying as to a mazer (wooden cup) that had been stolen
- Enhancing the market
- Practising the Art Magic
- For placing a certain piece of iron in a loaf of bread
- Cutting off a baselard (short sword); and Abjuration of the City
- A false seizure of ale
- False bow-strings
- Upon one who feigned himself a holy hermit
- Upon three men, counterfeiters of the Seal of his lordship the Pope, and of others, Lords of England
- Upon Laurence Neuport, who exposed divers counterfeit Papal Bulls.

CRAFTS IN LONDON, 1422

Mercers, merchants dealing in many articles, particularly textiles

Grocers, their forerunners being the Pepperers. They dealt in 'gross', in bulk, in spices and drugs

Drapers, exporters and importers of cloth

Fishmongers

Goldsmiths

Vintners, wine merchants

Skinners, controlled the fur trade

Tailors

Saddlers

Ironmongers

Girdlers, belt makers

Cordwainers, shoemakers who worked cordovan or cordwain, goatskin leather, originally from Cordoba in Spain

Haberdashers, an offshoot of the Mercers, later with two branches: the Hurers or Cappers who made and sold headgear, and the Milliners who imported fancy goods from Milan. In Elizabethan times they were particularly noted for the importation of pins.

Cutlers

Armourers

Weavers of Wool

Weavers of linen

Fullers, scourers and beaters of cloth as a means of cleaning and finishing it.

Dyers

Plasterers

Carpenters

Pewterers

Plumbers

Joiners

Founders, metal casters

Leathersellers

Bakers

Shearmen, cloth finishers

Lorimers, makers of the metal parts of horse harness

Waxchandlers

Tallowchandlers

Tanners

Curriers, dressers of tanned leather

Pouchmakers

Bowyers

Fletchers, arrow makers

Horners

Spurriers, makers of spurs

Hatters

Cofferers, makers of coffers

Pointmakers, points being the cords or strings used to attach one part of apparel to another

Wiremakers

Cardmakers, makers of combs for carding or combing wool or flax

Pinners

Whittawyers, harness makers

Leather-dyers

Stainers

Hostillers, inn-keepers

Cooks

Piemakers

Bellmakers

Corsours, horse-dealers

Chariotmakers

Broochmakers

Jewellers

Paternosters, makers of rosaries

Turners

Bookbinders

Writers of texts

Stationers

Poulters

Clockmakers

Chapemakers, makers of the metal ends for scabbards

Sheders, combers

Malemakers, makers of trunks

Tablemakers

Lockyers

Fourbours, polishers

Burlesters [?]

Lateners, brass-workers

Potters

Stuffers

Fruiterers

Cheesemongers

Stringers
Basketmakers
Barbers
Brewers
Butchers
Tapicers, tapestry
makers
Broderers
Painters
Salters, importers of
salt, flax, hemp and
chemicals such as
potash
Brasiers, brass workers
Smiths
Hurers, cap makers

Woodmongers
Writers of Court letters
Limners, artists
Leches, doctors
Ferours, ironworkers
Coppersmiths
Upholders,
upholsterers
Galochemakers, clog
and wooden
shoemakers
Carvers
Glassiers
Felmongers, dealers in
skins
Woolmen

Cornmongers
Blacksmiths
Ropers
Lanternmakers
Haymongers
Bottlemakers
Marblers
Netmakers
Potmakers
Glovers
Hosiers
Orglemakers, organ
makers
Soapmakers

THE TWELVE GREAT LIVERY COMPANIES of the City of London are, in order of precedence: the Mercers, Grocers, Drapers, Fishmongers, Goldsmiths, Skinners, Merchant Taylors (makers of tents and padded linen tunics worn under armour), Haberdashers, Salters, Ironmongers, Vintners, Clothworkers (an amalgamation of the Fullers and Shearmen). The Skinners and Merchant Taylors were in dispute over their rankings until the Lord Mayor ruled in 1484 that they should alternate between 6th and 7th places annually and entertain each other regularly. His intervention was very necessary: in 1340 an affray over precedence between the Skinners and the Fishmongers had resulted in loss of life.

SHEEP AND GROATS:
CURRENCIES AND THE WOOL TRADE

For much of the Middle Ages England's most important export was the summer wool clip and the autumn fells or sheepskins, with some 30,000 sacks being shipped each year at the highest point. Perhaps the biggest problem connected with the trade was the multitude of different currencies in which payments were made. For example:

> Andrew guilder of Scotland
> Arnoldus gulden of Gueldres
> Carolus groat of Charles of Burgundy
> New crowns and old crowns of France
> David and the Falewe of the Bishopric of Utrecht
> Hettinus groat of the Counts of Westphalia

Lewe or Louis d'Or
Limburg groat
Milan groat
Nimuegen groat
Phelippus or Philippe d'Or of Brabant
Plaques of Utrecht
Postlates of various bishops
English ryall (worth ten shillings)
Scots rider (bore figure of a horseman)
Burgundy rider
Florin Rhenau of the Bishopric of Cologne and the Setillers

English Cistercians' wool paid much of Richard I's ransom when he was imprisoned in Austria on the way home from the Third Crusade. Until the 14th century the trade was in the hands of the Italians but in 1354 the Fellowship of the STAPLE was incorporated, under a mayor, to handle all wool exports. This greatly eased the collection of duties on them, which formed a very large part of the royal income. The king could also look to the Staplers for loans secured against future duties. The Staple was located at Bruges, Antwerp, Calais and sometimes in England, until it came to rest at Calais in 1392. Dick Whittington, thrice mayor of London, was also a considerable wool exporter and twice mayor of the Staple. The Staplers typically bought the wool directly themselves in the Welsh borders (from Tintern Abbey in particular), Shropshire, Herefordshire, the Cotswolds, Yorkshire and Lincolnshire, or from BROGGERS, middlemen between the sheep farmers and the Staplers. The wool was shipped to Calais from London and the Medway ports and once ashore it was sold by the Staplers not only in Calais but at the fairs of Flanders and Brabant. In the 15th century wool exports were only averaging 10,000 sacks a year, the reason being that English cloth manufacturing was growing apace, and the Staplers were yielding pride of place to the MERCHANT ADVENTURERS who exported the cloth.

Anglia: I Mons, 2 Pons, 3 Fons, 4 Ecclesia, 5 Foemina, 6 Lana
For mountains, bridges, rivers, churches fair,
Women and wool, England's past compare.

I pray to God and Saint Oswold,
To bring the sheep safe back to fold.
The Shepherd's Prayer

I thank God and ever shall –
It is the sheep hath payed for all.
Inscription erected by John Barton, Stapler,
of Holme near Newark, Notts

BADGES OF THE GREAT MEDIEVAL FAMILIES

Badges were not the same as heraldic coats of arms or heraldic crests, though they could in time be adopted as crests, while some derived from coats of arms. They were often used as identifying marks or 'cognizances' on the clothing of retainers and adherents of the families, as well as on such items as horse trappings and furniture. They are particularly associated with the period of the Wars of the Roses in the fifteenth century and some have survived to the present day in municipal heraldry and inn signs.

ROYAL BADGES

HENRY II, RICHARD I, JOHN, HENRY III – the Planta Genista, broom plant, hence the name Plantagenet.

EDWARD I – Gold Rose. Edward's brother Edmund Crouchback used a Red Rose and in due course that became the badge of the House of Lancaster, while the White Rose (possibly derived from the Mortimer family) became the badge of the Yorkists.

EDWARD II – Castle, derived from his mother, Eleanor of Castile.

EDWARD III – Sunburst, Stock of a Tree (from Royal palace of Woodstock), a Falcon (of the Plantagenets), a Griffin, a Boar, Ostrich Feathers. There is no evidence for the story that the feathers were the badge or coat of arms of the King of Bohemia killed at Crecy fighting for the French. Edward's son, the Black Prince, used them on a black shield and this is the explanation for his nickname. Feathers or a feather continued to be used by a number of Lancastrian and Yorkist kings and it was only in Tudor times that they became particularly associated with the heir to the throne. (These are only some of the badges associated with Edward III. They continued to be used by his successors but are not repeated below.)

RICHARD II – White Hart, lodged (in a resting position), ducally gorged (with a ducal coronet round its neck) and chained.

HENRY IV – Monogram SS.

HENRY V – Chained Antelope. (See also Swan below.)

HENRY VI – Chained Antelope, Spotted Panther.

EDWARD IV – White Rose en Soleil, 'on the sun', also a collar alternating the sun with the white rose, a red and white rose en soleil referring to his marriage to Elizabeth Wydville of the Lancastrian Party, Black Bull (of Clarence), White Lion (of Mortimer), Falcon and Fetterlock (of York). (Again, these are only some of the badges associated with Edward IV.)

RICHARD III – White Boar, a Falcon with a Virgin's face holding a White Rose.

HENRY VII – Crowned Hawthorn bush (Richard III's crown was found under one at the Battle of Bosworth), Portcullis, badge of the Beaufort family from which his mother came, used in conjunction with Henry IV's SS monogram in chains, the White-and-Red Tudor Rose, the Red Dragon (of Cadwallader), the White Greyhound (of Richmond), the Yale (of Beaufort – a mythical animal with the appearance of a goat and the grace of a deer).

During the reign of Richard III a seditious rhyme was fastened to the door of St Paul's Cathedral:

> The Cat, the Rat and Lovell our dog
> Rule all England under an Hog.

The hog was Richard's own badge of a white boar, while the first line referred to his three henchmen: William Catesby, Sir Richard Ratcliffe and Lord Lovell, whose badge was a silver dog.

NOBLE BADGES

SILVER STAR – De Vere, Earls of Oxford. Confusion between this badge and the white rose en soleil caused the Lancastrians to lose the Battle of Barnet in 1471.

SWAN – De Bohun, Earls of Hereford The swan is ducally gorged and chained. Adopted by Henry V since his mother was one of two co-heiresses of the De Bohun family. The Stafford Dukes of Buckingham, descendants of the other heiress, also used the swan.

BEAR AND RAGGED STAFF – Beauchamp, Earls of Warwick. The ingredients began as separate badges. Richard Neville, Earl of Warwick, 'The Kingmaker', inherited by marrying the heiress of the last Beauchamp earl. It was also used by the sixteenth-century Dudley Earls of Warwick and Leicester.

ACORN, SWALLOW (Fr hirondelle) – Arundel

GOLD MOLET (rowel of spur) – Clinton

RED HEART – Douglas

WHITE LION – Howard

GREYHOUND (Fr *levrier*) – Mauleverer

MULBERRY TREE – Mowbray

BUCKLE – Pelham

SILVER CRESCENT, DOUBLE MANACLE – Percy, Earls of Northumberland

CORNISH CHOUGH (bird) – Scrope

TALBOT (hound) – Talbot, Earls of Shrewsbury

INTERLACED CORDS, KNOTS – Earls of Stafford, Dukes of Buckingham

'Time hath his revolutions; there must be a period and an end to all temporal things, finis rerum, an end of names and dignities and whatsoever is terrene; and why not of de Vere? – For where is Bohun? Where is Mowbray? Where is Mortimer? Nay, what is more and most of all where Plantagenet? They are entombed in the urns and sepulchres of mortality.' *Chief Justice Sir Ranulphe Crewe giving judgment in the de Vere inheritance case, 1625.*

Tudor rose

Seal of Richard Beauchamp
fifth Earl of Warwick d. 1439
showing the bear and
ragged staff

Badge of Catherine
of Aragon – half rose,
half pomegranate

White Hart
Badge of Richard II

Sunburst Badge
of Richard II

MEDIEVAL FALCONRY: A PECKING ORDER

A list of the falcons and hawks appropriate to various ranks of medieval society, from the fifteenth-century *Boke of St Albans*. As the notes below show, it is not quite so straightforward as it might appear.

Emperor .... Eagle, Vulture and Merloun
King .... Ger Falcon and the Tercel of the Ger Falcon
Prince .... Falcon Gentle and Tercel Gentle
Duke .... Falcon of the Loch
Earl .... Falcon Peregrine
Baron .... Bustard
Knight .... Sacre and Sacret
Esquire .... Lanere and Laneret
Lady .... Marlyon
Young Man .... Hobby
Yeoman .... Goshawk
Poor Man .... Jercel
Priest .... Sparrowhawk
Holy Water Clerk .... Musket
Knave or Servant .... Kestrel

EAGLE, VULTURE, MERLOUN – Neither of the first two is much use for falconry. Merloun is a variant spelling for merlin (see below).

GER FALCON AND TERCEL OF THE GER FALCON – The ger or gyr falcon comes from the sub-Arctic belt, e.g. Norway and Iceland. These days a tercel is the peregrine falcon male and the gyr falcon male is called a jerkin.

FALCON GENTLE – another name for the female peregrine.

FALCON OF THE LOCH – another name for the peregrine.

BUSTARD – not a bird of prey. Perhaps a mis-spelling for buzzard or for French *busard* (harrier).

SACRE AND SACRET – Saker and Sakret (male) from central Europe and central Asia.

LANERE AND LANERET – Lanner and Lanneret (male) from Africa and coastal mountains north of the Mediterranean.

MARLYON – another variant of merlin, the smallest of the falcons. The male is called a jack. Native to Britain.

HOBBY – the male is called a robin. Native to Britain.

GOSHAWK – the male is called a tiercel goshawk. Native to Britain.

JERCEL – this is a mystery: not in the *Oxford English Dictionary*.

SPARROWHAWK – native to Britain.

MUSKET – the male sparrowhawk.

KESTREL – native to Britain.

Gyrfalcons, peregrines and launers (lanners) in fact seem to have been the principal falcons flown by English royalty and aristocracy; as to hawks, it was the goshawk and the sparrowhawk. The hunting style of hawks is low-flying, while falcons 'stoop', diving on their prey from a height.

THE TUDORS

TUDOR VICTIMS

The ruthlessness of the Tudors is epitomised for many by Henry VIII's execution of two of his wives and by his daughter Mary's burning of Protestants at the stake. But those with most to fear from Henry VII, his son and grandchildren, had Yorkist or other strains of royal blood in their veins, and this included even Tudor blood if it came through female lines.

The Yorkists, descended from Edward III's son, Edmund Duke of York, were the losers in the Wars of the Roses, when Richard III was killed at the battle of Bosworth in 1485 and the crown went to Henry Tudor, Henry VII, who was of rather tenuous Lancastrian descent, from John of Gaunt, Duke of Lancaster – another of Edward III's sons. But only with hindsight can Bosworth be seen as the decisive victory for the new Royal House. Fear of a renewed descent into the horrors of civil war, because of a challenge from a pretender or a disputed succession, lay behind the severity with which possible claimants were handled and the longing for male heirs. These feelings were shared by the majority of Tudor Englishmen and women, and the troubled period which followed the death of Henry VIII in 1547 and lasted until Elizabeth came to the throne in 1558 amply justified them.

After Bosworth Henry VII was quick to marry Elizabeth, daughter of Richard III's brother and predecessor, Edward IV, in an attempt to increase the amount of Plantagenet blood that would run in his children's veins. It has been claimed that this was a futile exercise since Edward IV could not in fact have been the son of Richard, Duke of York. Given that Edward was born on 28 April 1442 he must have been conceived at a time in 1441 when Richard was not in Rouen with his wife Cicely (née Neville) but off by himself on campaign in Pontoise. It has also been pointed out how often Yorkist supporters emphasised Edward IV's legitimacy.

Henry VII lost no time in executing Richard III's bastard JOHN OF PONTEFRACT and in consigning EDWARD, EARL OF WARWICK, son of another of Richard's brothers, the Duke of Clarence, to the Tower of London, although he was only ten years old. Within a year or two Lambert Simnel was impersonating Warwick well enough for the inhabitants of Dublin to crown him. Simnel, together with JOHN, EARL OF LINCOLN, eldest son of Richard III's sister Elizabeth, then had to be confronted and defeated by Henry VII at the battle of Stoke in 1487. Warwick spent 14 years in the Tower until another attempt at impersonating him in 1499 persuaded Henry that he was too much of a liability to remain alive, so he was beheaded.

EDMUND, EARL OF SUFFOLK, a brother of the Earl of Lincoln defeated and killed at Stoke, was actively plotting against Henry in the early 1500s. He and one brother, Richard, escaped to the Continent, but another, WILLIAM DE LA POLE, went to the Tower and remained there until he apparently died of natural causes in 1539. Called THE WHITE ROSE after the Yorkist badge, Edmund was handed over captive to Henry by Philip of Burgundy in 1506 and he then joined his brother William in the Tower. Henry made a solemn pledge not to execute him, but instructed his son to do so as soon as he came to the throne. In fact Henry VIII waited until he went to war with France in 1513, when the French king, Louis XII, recognised the other de la Pole brother Richard as king of England. This was enough to ensure that Edmund went to the block.

EDWARD STAFFORD, DUKE OF BUCKINGHAM was descended from neither John Duke of Lancaster nor Edmund Duke of York but from their brother Thomas of Woodstock (all three being sons of Edward III). Also his mother, Catherine Wydville, was the sister of Edward IV's queen. Buckingham was too proud of his royal connections for his own good, insulting Henry VIII's parvenu chief minister, Cardinal Wolsey, and speculating about his own prospects if no royal male heir was born. He was executed in 1521. 'That which ruineth the World, ruined him, his tongue.' (His father had been executed in 1483, while his grandfather, great-grandfather and great-great-grandfather were all slain in the Wars of the Roses.)

In 1538 HENRY COURTENAY, MARQUIS OF EXETER and HENRY POLE, LORD MONTAGUE were arraigned for treason, largely on the word of the latter's brother, Sir Geoffrey Pole, who had turned king's evidence to save his own skin. Exeter was the son of Edward IV's daughter Katherine while Montague's mother Margaret, Countess of Salisbury was a daughter of Edward's brother, the Duke of Clarence. Both men lacked enthusiasm for the changes the king was bringing about in religious matters and had behaved equivocally at the time of the rising known as the Pilgrimage of Grace. Henry told the French ambassador that he had long intended to extinguish the House of the White Rose. Both died on Tower Green in 1538, Montague's end being hastened when another brother, Cardinal Reginald Pole, was sent on a mission by the Pope to rouse the King of France and the Emperor Charles V against Henry. Exeter's son Edward (later Earl of Devon) went to the Tower at the same time as his father and was only released in 1553.

MARGARET, COUNTESS OF SALISBURY, who had been in the Tower since her son Montague's arrest in 1538, was hacked to death by an apprentice executioner in 1441, in spite of her age and the fact that she had been the best friend of Henry VIII's first wife Catherine of Aragon and acted as a second mother to her daughter Mary Tudor.

ARTHUR PLANTAGENET, VISCOUNT LISLE, was the illegitimate son of Edward IV, holding the important post of Lord Deputy of Calais, which still belonged to England. In 1540 he was sent to the Tower on a charge of plotting to surrender the town trumped up by Thomas Cromwell, Henry's chief minister in succession to Wolsey, who was himself struggling to maintain his position. It is true that Lisle's chaplain had been in touch with Cardinal Pole, but that was all, and Cromwell was merely using a false accusation to ingratiate himself with his master. Lisle was not brought to trial because Cromwell himself fell from power and was executed. However, he died in 1542, before regaining his freedom.

HENRY HOWARD, EARL OF SURREY was the hothead son of the 3rd Duke of Norfolk, and a poet. The Howards claimed royal descent from Thomas of Brotherton, fifth son of Edward I. In 1547 Surrey was foolish enough to add the arms of Edward the Confessor (azure a cross fleury between five martlets or) to his own coat of arms. This provided an excuse for his arrest and execution, though he had also ill-advisedly promoted the claims of his father to become Protector to the future child-King, Edward VI. (His own son, the 4TH DUKE OF NORFOLK, was to be executed in 1572 for plotting to establish Mary Queen of Scots on the English throne.)

Shortly before his death in 1553, Edward VI was persuaded by the most powerful figure of the day, JOHN DUDLEY, DUKE OF NORTHUMBERLAND, to make a will cutting his half-sisters Mary and Elizabeth out of the succession and giving it instead to LADY JANE GREY, who was married to Northumberland's son, GUILFORD DUDLEY. (John Dudley's father, EDMUND DUDLEY, had been executed by the young Henry VIII in 1510, the first of the many judicial murders during his reign. His crime was to have been, together with Sir Richard Empson, also executed in 1510, the instrument of Henry VII's grasping and avaricious policies in the latter years of his reign.) Lady Jane Grey's grandmother was Mary Tudor, a sister of Henry VIII. On Edward VI's death Jane reigned for nine days before being deposed by the other Mary Tudor, half-sister of Edward, to whom the vast majority of the population remained loyal. The Duke of Northumberland was executed almost immediately, but Lady Jane and her husband lingered until the following year when the abortive rebellion of Sir Thomas Wyatt made up Mary's mind that it was too much of a risk to let them live. Lady Jane's father, HENRY GREY, DUKE OF SUFFOLK, and his brother THOMAS GREY were also executed in 1554.

In 1557, THOMAS STAFFORD, grandson of the Duke of Buckingham executed in 1521 and whose mother was Ursula Pole, a daughter of the Countess of Salisbury executed in 1541, foolishly raised once more his family's claim to the throne. Worse still, the French king chose to support his claim, so he too went to the block

The final name in this melancholy catalogue is that of MARY, QUEEN OF SCOTS. She had Tudor blood via her grandmother Margaret and once she fled to England in 1568 she became the focus for a series of Catholic plots to put her in Queen Elizabeth's place. Finally, with the greatest reluctance, Elizabeth signed her death warrant in 1587 and she was executed at Fotheringay Castle.

The beheading of Lady Jane Grey in the Tower

TUDOR VICTIMS

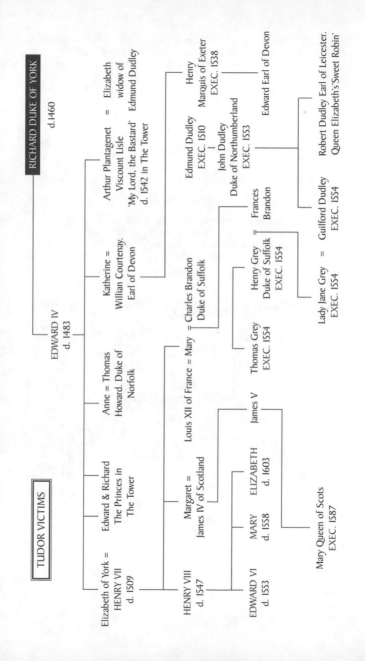

RICHARD DUKE OF YORK
d.1460

EDWARD IV
d. 1483

Elizabeth of York = HENRY VII
d. 1509

Edward & Richard
The Princes in
The Tower

Anne = Thomas
Howard. Duke of
Norfolk

Katherine = William Courtenay.
Earl of Devon

Arthur Plantagenet
Viscount Lisle
'My Lord, the Bastard'
d. 1542 in The Tower

= Elizabeth
widow of
Edmund Dudley

Henry
Marquis of Exeter
EXEC. 1538

Edmund Dudley
EXEC. 1510
John Dudley
Duke of Northumberland
EXEC. 1553

Edward Earl of Devon

HENRY VIII
d. 1547

Margaret = James IV of Scotland

Louis XII of France = Mary = Charles Brandon
Duke of Suffolk

Frances
Brandon

Robert Dudley Earl of Leicester.
Queen Elizabeth's 'Sweet Robin'

Guilford Dudley
EXEC. 1554

EDWARD VI
d. 1553

MARY
d. 1558

ELIZABETH
d. 1603

James V

Thomas Grey
EXEC. 1554

Henry Grey
Duke of Suffolk
EXEC. 1554

Lady Jane Grey
EXEC. 1554

= Guilford Dudley
EXEC. 1554

Mary Queen of Scots
EXEC. 1587

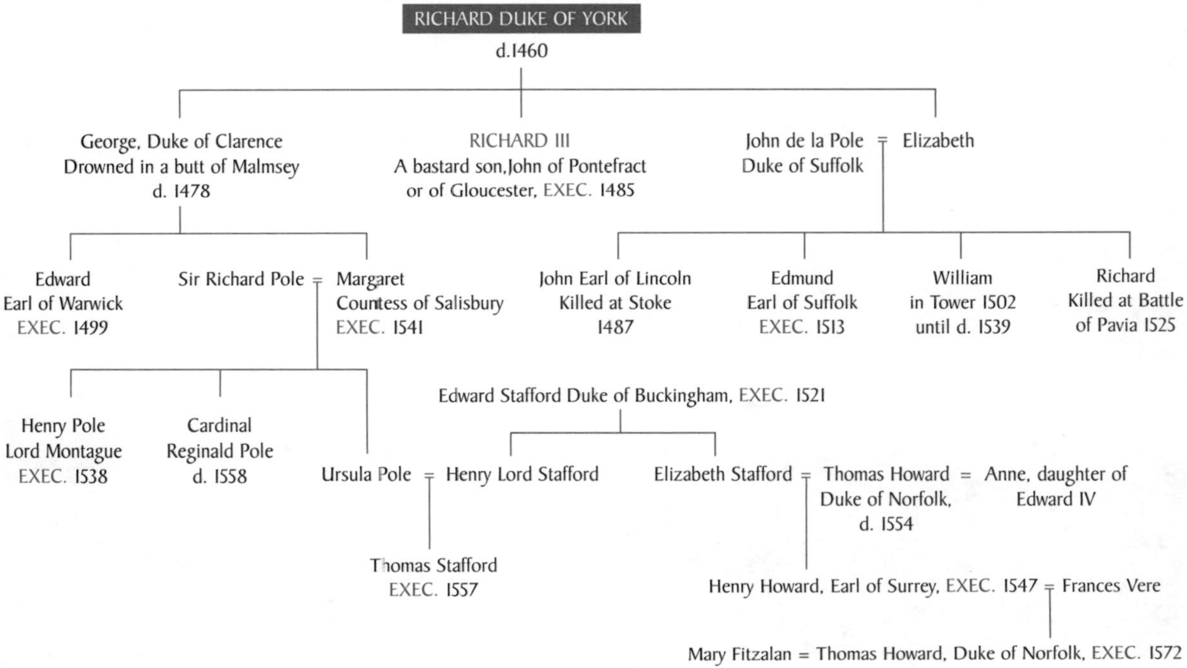

RICHARD DUKE OF YORK
d.1460

George, Duke of Clarence
Drowned in a butt of Malmsey
d. 1478

RICHARD III
A bastard son, John of Pontefract
or John of Gloucester, EXEC. 1485

John de la Pole = Elizabeth
Duke of Suffolk

Edward
Earl of Warwick
EXEC. 1499

Sir Richard Pole = Margaret
Countess of Salisbury
EXEC. 1541

John Earl of Lincoln
Killed at Stoke
1487

Edmund
Earl of Suffolk
EXEC. 1513

William
in Tower 1502
until d. 1539

Richard
Killed at Battle
of Pavia 1525

Henry Pole
Lord Montague
EXEC. 1538

Cardinal
Reginald Pole
d. 1558

Ursula Pole = Henry Lord Stafford

Edward Stafford Duke of Buckingham, EXEC. 1521

Thomas Stafford
EXEC. 1557

Henry Lord Stafford

Elizabeth Stafford = Thomas Howard
Duke of Norfolk,
d. 1554

Anne, daughter of
Edward IV

Henry Howard, Earl of Surrey, EXEC. 1547 = Frances Vere

Mary Fitzalan = Thomas Howard, Duke of Norfolk, EXEC. 1572

THE SCALDING HOUSE AND THE GROOM OF THE STOOL: THE TUDOR COURT

Government in the 16th century was a personal affair with the Monarch by far the most important element, the centrepiece, focus and fount. Therefore the frame surrounding the Monarchy, the Royal Court, had to be large and elaborate, especially since both Henry VIII and Elizabeth wished to be seen as in the same league as the kings of France and Spain, both far bigger and richer countries. At times the Court was absorbing a third of all the Crown's ordinary revenue, not primarily because of profligacy and self-indulgence but because it was such an important adjunct of kingship that expense could not be spared if the right effect was to be achieved. There were also about 175 posts at Court 'worth a gentleman's having', so about half the nobility and one-fifth of the major gentry families could expect a position for one or more family members. This made the Court an important adhesive, holding together the fabric of the realm.

The first division within the Court was between the Household proper and those departments outside it, with their own fixed locations; some were at the Tower of London, while the GREAT WARDROBE, dealing with cloth and clothing, was at Baynard's Castle in the City. (A TOYLE or Toil House was where nets, traps, snares, falcons, hawks and other hunting equipment were kept.) Within the Household, there were two main divisions: the Domus Regie Magnificencie consisting of the Chamber and the Privy Chamber, and answering to the LORD CHAMBERLAIN; and the Domus Providencie or service division, answering to the LORD STEWARD.

Within the Domus Providencie, the GREAT HALL was something of a medieval relic and by Elizabeth's reign it was a dead letter. SEWERS supervised service and seating at table; the KNIGHT MARSHAL policed the Court and carried out the judgements of the Lord Steward; the CHAUNDRY provided candles; the EWERY provided water; the ALMONRY dispensed alms to the poor and deserving; the ACATRY was responsible for meat; the SCALDING HOUSE was where poultry and game were plucked and drawn. In 1558 there were 290 working under the Lord Steward. A major priority was to produce an impression of magnificence, which inevitably led to extravagance and waste. There were valuable perquisites for officers, such as lees of wine, candle ends, offal, crusts, etc.

The days when the CHAMBER was a solitary room behind the dais in the Great Hall, to which the king could retire, were long gone. There were suites of rooms with an elaborate hierarchy of attendants, but by the time of the death of Henry VII in 1509, the need for more seclusion was becoming pressing and was met by the establishment of the PRIVY CHAMBER. Within the Chamber the 'GUARD' were the Yeomen of the Guard first recruited by Henry VII in 1485, while the GENTLEMEN PENSIONERS were a guard of honour established in 1539 (today's Gentlemen at Arms). By 1520 the chief gentleman of the Privy Chamber was a powerful figure, claiming to be independent of the Lord Chamberlain, even though in origin his job as GROOM OF THE STOOL was to look after Henry VIII's lavatory. Elizabeth naturally required women body servants to attend her so the Privy Chamber became a female department and in consequence lost power and importance to the Privy Council, but the Court as a whole remained of vital importance as the stage setting in which the queen could play out her role as Gloriana, as she progressed between such royal residences as Richmond, Greenwich, Windsor, Hampton Court or Eltham (by the end of her Father's reign there had been 55 royal palaces), and the private houses of her leading subjects.

As a postscript to the Tudor Court, it is worth recalling that Katharine of Valois, the widow of Henry V and only 21 when he died, fell in love with her Welsh Clerk of the Wardrobe, Owen Tudor, and later married him before giving birth to Edmund Tudor, the father of the first Tudor king, Henry VII.

THE STUCTURE OF THE TUDOR COURT

DEPARTMENTS OUTSIDE THE HOUSEHOLD

STABLES
Master of the Horse
KENNELS
Masters of the Hounds
TOYLES
Sergeant Falconer
GREAT WARDROBE
Master
TENTS AND REVELS
Master
CHAPEL ROYAL ——— CHORISTERS
Dean   Master
JEWEL HOUSE
Master
WORKS
Clerk
ORDNANCE
Master
ROYAL BARGE

Keepers of Palaces

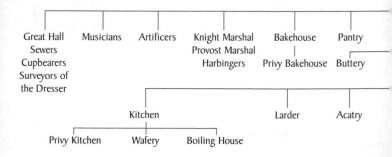

Great Hall	Musicians	Artificers	Knight Marshal	Bakehouse	Pantry
Sewers			Provost Marshal		
Cupbearers			Harbingers	Privy Bakehouse	Buttery
Surveyors of					
the Dresser					

Kitchen   Larder   Acatry

Privy Kitchen   Wafery   Boiling House

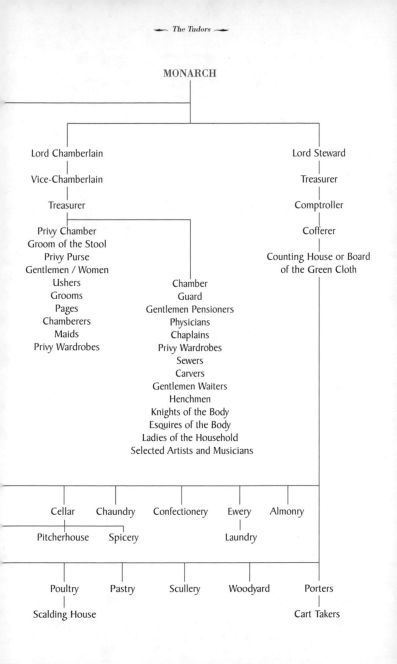

MONARCH

Lord Chamberlain

Vice-Chamberlain

Treasurer

Privy Chamber
Groom of the Stool
Privy Purse
Gentlemen / Women
Ushers
Grooms
Pages
Chamberers
Maids
Privy Wardrobes

Chamber
Guard
Gentlemen Pensioners
Physicians
Chaplains
Privy Wardrobes
Sewers
Carvers
Gentlemen Waiters
Henchmen
Knights of the Body
Esquires of the Body
Ladies of the Household
Selected Artists and Musicians

Lord Steward

Treasurer

Comptroller

Cofferer

Counting House or Board
of the Green Cloth

Cellar   Chaundry   Confectionery   Ewery   Almonry

Pitcherhouse   Spicery   Laundry

Poultry   Pastry   Scullery   Woodyard   Porters

Scalding House   Cart Takers

DUNG AND GOUNG:
LONDON STREET NUISANCES IN 1562

In his *Survey of London*, the great Tudor historian of the city, John Stow, reproduced a tract which listed 'such statutes for keeping the streets clean as are still in force'.

• No man shall sweep the filth of the street into the channel of the City, in the time of any rain, or at any other time, under pain of six shillings and eight pence.

• No man shall cast or lay in the streets dogs, cats or other carrion, or any noisome thing, contagious of air. Nor any innholder shall lay out dung out of his house, but if the carr be ready to carry the same away incontinently, under pain of forty shillings.

• No man shall ride or drive his car or cart atrot in the street, but patiently, under pain of two shillings.

• No man shall gallop his horse in the street, under pain of two shillings.

• No man shall shoot in the street for wager, or otherwise, under like pain of two shillings.

• No man shall bowl, or cast any stone in the street, for wager, or gain, or such-like, under pain of two shillings.

• No man shall dig any hole in the street for any matter, except he stop it up again, under pain of two shillings, and recompence to any person hurt thereby, two shillings.

• No man shall bury any dung, or goung [a privy, or its contents], within the liberties of this City, under pain of forty shillings.

• No goungfermour shall carry any ordure till after nine of the clock in the night, under pain of thirteen shillings four pence.

• No man shall have any kine, goats, hogs, pigs, hens, cocks, capons, or ducks, in the open street, under pain of forfeiture of the same.

• No man shall maintain any biting curs, or mad dogs, in the streets, under pain of two shillings, and recompence unto every party hurt therewith, two shillings.

• No man shall blow any horn in the night within this City, or whistle after the hour of nine o'clock in the night, under pain of imprisonment.

• No man shall use to go with vizards, or disguised by night, under like pain of imprisonment.

• That night-walkers and eaves-droppers endure like punishment.

• No hammer-men, as a smith, a pewterer, a founder, and all artificers making great sound, shall not work after the hour of nine in the night, nor afore the hour of four in the morning, under pain of three shillings four pence.

• No man shall go in the streets by night or by day with bow bent, or arrows under his girdle, nor with sword unscabbered, under pain of imprisonment; or with hand-gun, having therewith powder and match, except it be an usual May-game and sight.

• No butcher shall sell any measle hog, or unwholesome flesh, under pain of ten pounds.

• No butcher shall sell any old stale victuals, that is to say, above the slaughter of three days in the winter, and two in the summer, under pain of ten pounds.

• No victualler of this City shall give any rude or unfitting language or make any clamour upon any man or woman in the open market, for cheapening of victual, under pain of three shillings four pence.

• No man shall cast any urine-boles, or ordure-boles into the street by day or night, afore the hour of nine in the night; and also he shall not cast it out, but bring it down, and lay it in the canel, under pain of three shillings four pence; and, if he do cast it upon any person's head, the person to have a lawful recompence, if he have hurt thereby.

THE OPENING OF PARLIAMENT, 1563

In this account from the early years of Queen Elizabeth's reign it is possible to detect a number of elements that survive in today's State Openings of Parliament: the Sword and Cap of Maintenance carried before the monarch, the Gentlemen at Arms (Pensioners) and the Yeomen of the Guard (Guard), the Lord Chancellor on the Woolsack (though there appear to have been four Sacks in those days), noblemen's sons sitting on the steps round the throne, the summoning of the Commons to the Lords. The order of procession incidentally demonstrates the modest size of the peerage, with only one duke and two marquises.

Sir Edward Rogers was Comptroller of the Royal Household; Sir Nicholas Bacon was both Lord Keeper of the Great Seal and Lord Chancellor; Clarencieux, Norroy and Garter were kings-of-arms; a caul was a close-fitting woman's cap; Lord Robert Dudley, the Queen's favourite, was created Earl of Leicester the following year; St Edward's Staff was surmounted by an orb containing a fragment of the true cross; Lord Hunsdon was the son of Anne Boleyn's sister and so first cousin of the Queen – some said he was her half-brother because Anne's sister was also mistress of Henry VIII; a traverse was a small curtained-off area; the Cloth of State was a canopy over the Queen; Dr Huicke was one of the Queen's physicians.

• On Tuesday the 12th day of January ... about eleven of the clock in the forenoon, the Queen's Majesty took her horse at the Hall door and proceeded in manner as followeth:

• First, all GENTLEMEN, two and two, then ESQUIRES, KNIGHTS, and BANNERETS, and LORDS BEING NO BARONS OR UNDER AGE.

• Then the TRUMPETERS sounding.

• Then the QUEEN'S SERJEANT, Mr Carus, in his surcoat, hood, and mantle unlined of scarlet.

• Then Mr Gerard, the QUEEN'S ATTORNEY, and Mr Russell, SOLICITOR.

• Then Anthony Browne and Mr Weston, JUSTICES OF THE COMMON PLEAS.

• Then the BARONS OF THE EXCHEQUER.

• Then Mr Corbet and Mr Whiddon, two JUSTICES OF THE KING'S BENCH.

• Then Sir Thomas Saunders, CHIEF BARON OF THE EXCHEQUER, and Sir James Dyer, CHIEF JUSTICE OF THE COMMON PLEAS.

• Then Sir William Cordell, MASTER OF THE ROLLS, in his gown and Sir Robert Catlin, CHIEF JUSTICE OF THE KING'S BENCH; and these Justices and Barons of the Exchequer in their scarlet mantles, hood, and surcoat edged with miniver, the mantle shorter than the surcoat by a foot.

• Then KNIGHTS Councillors in their gowns.

• Then Sir William Cecil, CHIEF SECRETARY and Sir Edward Rogers, COMPTROLLER.

• Then William Howard, bearing the QUEEN'S CLOAK AND HAT.

• Then the BARONS, in all 40 but there in number 30 ... their mantles, hoods, and surcoats furred, and two rows of miniver on their right shoulder.

• Then proceeded the BISHOPS, all that were there present were but 22 ... their robes of scarlet lined, and a hood down their back of miniver.

• Then the VISCOUNTS, their robes as the Barons, but that they had two rows and an half of miniver, as the Viscount of Bindon absent, Viscount Montague and Viscount Hereford present.

• Then the EARLS, but 19 present ... their robes of scarlet with three rows of miniver.

• Then the MARQUIS of Winchester, but now as Lord Treasurer, and the Marquis of Northampton; the DUKE of Norfolk went as Earl Marshal.

• Then the LORD KEEPER'S SERJEANT AND SEAL, and after Sir Nicholas Bacon, LORD KEEPER OF THE GREAT SEAL, in his gown.

• Here CLARENCIEUX AND NORROY.

• Then the QUEEN'S SERJEANT-AT-ARMS, and after, GARTER.

• Then the Duke of Norfolk with the gilt rod as MARSHAL, the LORD TREASURER with the CAP OF ESTATE, and the Earl of Worcester with the SWORD.

• Then the QUEEN'S MAJESTY on horseback, a little behind the LORD CHAMBERLAIN and VICE-CHAMBERLAIN; her Grace apparelled in her mantle, opened before, furred with ermines, and her kirtle of crimson velvet, close before, and close sleeves, but the bands turned up with ermines, and a hood hanging low round about her neck of ermines. Over all a rich collar, set with stones and other jewels, and on her head a rich caul. And the next after her the Lord Robert Dudley, MASTER OF THE HORSE, leading the spare horse. And after all other ladies, two and two, in their ordinary apparel. Beside the Queen went her footmen, and along on either side of her went the PENSIONERS with their axes; after the ladies followed the CAPTAIN OF THE GUARD, Sir William St Loe, and after him the GUARD.

In which order her Majesty proceeded to the north door of the Church of Westminster, where the DEAN there and the DEAN OF THE CHAPEL [ROYAL] met her, and THE WHOLE CHAPEL in copes; and St Edward's staff with the inlet in the top was delivered unto her, her arm for the bearing thereof assisted by the Baron of Hunsdon; the Canopy borne over her by Charles Howard esquire (and 5 knights); her Grace's train borne up and assisted, for the weight thereof from her arms, by the Lord Robert Dudley, Master of the Horse, and Sir Francis Knollys, Vice-Chamberlain; and so orderly proceeded to the traverse beside the Table of Administration, although other Princes have used to be placed in the Choir till the Offering, but not now because there was neither Communion nor Offering. And so she being placed, all the Lords sat down on forms besides the traverse, the spiritualty on the north side and the temporalty on the south side; the Sword and the Cap of Estate laid down on the Table. Then the choir sung the English Procession; which ended, Mr Nowell, DEAN OF PAUL'S, began his sermon, and first made his prayer orderly for the Queen's Majesty and the Universal Church, and especially for that honourable Assembly of Three Estates there present, that they might make such laws as should be to God's glory and the good of the realm.

The sermon being ended and a psalm sung, her Majesty and the rest orderly on foot proceeded out of the south door, where she delivered the Dean the sceptre, and so proceeded into the Parliament Chamber, where the Queen stayed awhile in her Privy Chamber till all the Lords and others were placed, and then her Highness came forth and went and sat down in her Royal Place and Chair of Estate (the Sword and Cap of Maintenance borne before her) and when she stood up her mantle was assisted and borne up from her arms by the Lord Robert Dudley, Master of the Horse, and Sir Francis Kollys, Vice-Chamberlain.

The Lord Keeper sat alone upon the uppermost Sack until the Queen was sat, and then went and stood without the rail, on the right hand the Cloth of Estate;

and the Lord Treasurer, holding the Cap of Estate, on the right hand before the Queen, Garter standing by him, and on the left hand standing the Earl of Worcester with the Sword, and by him the Lord Chamberlain.

The Duke of Norfolk began the first form and the Viscount Montague (for that the Viscount Bindon was not there) ended it. The Lord Clinton, the Lord Admiral, began the form behind, that of the Barons, and the Lord St John of Bletsoe ended it. The Archbishop of Canterbury began the Bishops' form, and the Bishop of Gloucester ended the same.

[The judges and high civil servants sitting on three further Woolsacks are listed.]

At the side hand of the Queen sat on the ground three or four ladies and no more; and at the back of the rail, behind the Cloth of Estate, kneeled the Earls of Oxford and Rutland, under age, the Earl of Desmond, the Lord Roos, the Lord Herbert of Cardiff, and divers other noblemen's sons and heirs …

The Queen's Majesty, being set (as aforesaid) under the Cloth of Estate, the HOUSE OF COMMONS had notice thereof; and thereupon the KNIGHTS, CITIZENS AND BURGESSES of the same repaired to the Upper House, and being, as many as conveniently could, let in, she commanded Sir Nicholas Bacon, the Lord Keeper, to open the cause of calling and assembling this Parliament.

THE BORDER CLANS

From England's defeat of the Scottish army under James IV at the Battle of Flodden in 1513 until the accession of his great-grandson, James VI and I, to the English throne in 1603, the Anglo-Scottish border was a lawless place. It had not been particularly peaceable for the previous two hundred years, but the level of cattle thieving on both sides, of 'lifting and looting', of blackmail and kidnapping, reached new heights, just at a time when the rest of England was becoming more law-abiding. The clans or families of reivers, robbers, whose home territories are indicated on the accompanying map, 'shook loose the Border', harrying not only those opposite them across it but often their neighbours on the same side as well. The Border was divided into three – East, Middle and West – and both governments appointed Wardens of these Marches, who attempted to police matters. There was a measure of cooperation between the two sets of Wardens and one convention allowed what was called Hot Trod, the pursuit of reivers and stolen cattle across the Border by either side.

James VI and I had no hesitation in ruthlessly suppressing the reivers: 32 Elliots, Armstrongs, Johnstones and Batys (Beatties) were hung, 15 were banished and 140 were outlawed in 1603. If they got any justice, it was summary. Informers, searchers and sleuth hounds were employed to keep the hangman busy in subsequent years. Seeing which way the wind was blowing 2,000 Scots went off to fight as mercenaries under Walter Scott of Buccleuch against the Spanish in the Low Countries. By 1610 the Border was subdued.

THE ENGLISH AND SPANISH FLEETS IN 1588

'Her Majesty's whole army at the seas against the Spanish forces'

SHIP'S NAME	TONS	MEN	CAPTAIN
Ark	800	425	The Lord Admiral Lord Howard of Effingham
Elizabeth Bonaventure	600	350	Earl of Cumberland
Rainbow	500	250	Lord Henry Seymour
Golden Lion	500	250	Lord Thomas Howard
White Bear	1000	500	Lord Sheffield
Vanguard	500	250	Sir Wm Wynter
Revenge	500	250	Sir Francis Drake
Elizabeth Jonas	900	500	Sir Rbt Southwell
Victory	800	400	Sir John Hawkins
Antelope	400	160	Sir Henry Palmer
Triumph	1100	500	Sir Martin Frobisher
Dreadnought	400	200	Sir George Beeston
Mary Rose	600	250	Edward Fenton
Nonpareil	500	250	Thomas Fenner
Hope	600	250	Robert Crosse
Galley Bonavolia	0	250	William Borough
Swiftsure	400	180	Edward Fenner
Swallow	360	160	Richard Hawkins

Foresight	300	160	Chr. Baker
Aid	250	120	W. Fenner
Bull	200	100	Jeremy Turner
Tiger	200	100	John Bostocke
Tramontana	150	70	Luke Ward
Scout	120	70	Henry Ashley
Achates	100	60	Gregory Riggs
Charles	70	45	John Roberts
George Hoy	100	24	Rich. Hodges

[And seven vessels of less than 70 tons. The figures for men include mariners, gunners and soldiers.]

'There were besides: 34 merchants' ships with Sir Francis Drake, westward; 30 ships and barks paid by the City of London; 33 ships and barks with 15 victuallers, under the Lord Admiral; 20 coasters, great and small, under the Lord Admiral, paid by the Queen; 23 coasters, under Lord Henry Seymour, paid by the Queen; 23 voluntary ships, great and small. Totalis: 197 ships, 15,925 men.'

—— ENGLISH CANNON AT THE TIME OF THE ARMADA ——

'The secrets of the use of great ordnance'

	Height of the piece (inches)	Weight of the piece (lbs)	Weight of the shot (lbs)	Weight of the powder (lbs)
Cannon Royal	8⅓	7,000	66	30
Cannon	8	6,000	60	27
Cannon Serpentine	7½	5,500	53⅓	25
Bastard Cannon	7	4,500	41¼	20
Demi-Cannon	6½	4,000	30¼	18
Cannon Pedro	6	3,000	24¼	14
Culverin	5½	4,500	17½	12
Basilisco	5	4,000	15¼	10
Demi-Culverin	4½	3,400	9⅓	8
Bastard Culverin	4	3,000	7	6¼
Saker	3½	1,400	5⅓	5⅓
Minion	3¼	1,000	4	4
Falcon of 2⅓	2⅓	800	3	3
Falconet	2	500	1¼	1¼
Serpentine	1½	400	⅓	⅓
Robinet	1	300	⅓	⅓
Falcon	2½	660	2¼	2¼

The demi-cannon was something like the 18th-century carronade, throwing a heavy ball about 500 yards point-blank. The culverin was more like the conventional naval cannon with a point-blank range of 700 yards and at random (extreme range), about two miles. The small guns at the bottom of the list were designed to kill men, not cripple ships, and were often breech-loaded rather than muzzle-loaded.

———————— THE SPANISH ARMADA ————————

The table overleaf needs some explanation. The armadas of Portugal and Castile had ten first-line galleons each. The four galleasses of Naples were also rated in the first line. The second line was made up of four squadrons of ten large merchantmen each – from Biscay, Guipuzcoa, Andalusia, Levant (Venice, Ragusa-Dubrovnik, Genoa, Sicily, Barcelona). There were in fact thirty-four light, fast ships – zabras, patasses, fegatas, some being attached to the armadas. The hulks or urcas were bulky supply ships. The four galleys were from Portugal and not a lot of help.

	Ships	Tons	Guns	Soldiers	Mariners	Total
Armada of Portugal	12	7,737	347	3,330	1,293	4,623
Biscay	14	6,567	238	1,937	863	2,800
Castille	16	8,714	384	2,458	1,719	4,171
Andaluzia	11	8,762	240	2,327	780	3,105
Guipuscoa	14	6,991	247	1,992	616	2,608
Levant Ships	10	7,705	280	2,780	767	3,523
Hulks	23	10,271	384	3,121	608	3,729
Patasses and Zebras	22	1,121	91	479	574	1,093
Galleasses of Naples	4	—	200	773	468	1,341
Galleys	4	—	20	—	362	362
	130	57,868	2,431	19,295	8,050	27,365
Rowers						2,088
Summa Totalis						29,453

ELIZABETHAN MONOPOLIES

Arms of Sir Walter Raleigh

The justification for granting individuals monopolies in various products and processes was that they encouraged new inventions or protected what is now called intellectual property; they were also a means of rewarding those who had done the Monarch a particular service. Robert Cecil, son of Queen Elizabeth's chief minister, Lord Burghley, held them to be 'for the most part contentious and grievous to the subject, chiefly such as touch the poorer sort'. Monopolies remained contentious, and an Act against them was passed towards the end of James I's reign in 1624. In the 1630s Charles I resorted to various methods of raising money without summoning Parliament, and the granting of monopolies was one such device. In a debate on monopolies in the House of Commons in 1601 Robert Cecil listed all those granted since the 17th year (1574/5) of Elizabeth's reign. The great composers Thomas Tallis and William Byrd were granted a 21-year monopoly of publishing printed part-songs and lined manuscript music staff paper in January 1575, escaping inclusion in Cecil's list.

• TO ROBERT SPARKE, to make spangles and owes [hose?] of gold.

• TO SIR EDWARD DYER [poet and courtier], to pardon, dispense and release all forfeitures and abuses committed by tanners, contrary to the statute.

• TO WILLIAM WADE [or Waad, diplomatist, clerk of the Privy Council, investigator of Catholic plots] and others, for the making of sulphur, brimstone and oil.

• TO JAMES CHAMBERS, to give license for tanning, contrary to the statute.

• TO SIR WALTER RALEIGH, of tonnage and poundage [customs duties] of wines.

• TO WILLIAM WATKINS, to print almanacks.

• TO [UNKNOWN], to print David's Psalms.

• TO ONE KIRKE and others, to take the benefit of sowing flax and hemp.

• TO RICHARD WELCH, to print the History of Cornelius Tacitus.

• TO [UNKNOWN], to transport iron and tin.

• TO JOHN NORDEN, to print Speculum Britanniae [the pioneer mapmaker's great uncompleted project for a county-by-county history of England].

• TO [UNKNOWN], to print the Psalms of David, according to the Hebrew text.

• TO CERTAIN MERCHANTS, to traffic.

• TO SIR JEROME BOWES, to make glasses.

• TO [UNKNOWN], to provide and transport lists [the border, edging, selvage of cloth?] and shreds.

• TO HENRY NOEL [courtier], to make stone-pots, etc.

• TO WILLIAM ABER, to sow six hundred acres of ground with oade [woad?]

• TO MR HEALS, to provide steel beyond the seas.

• TO [UNKNOWN], to have one shilling upon every hogshead of pilchards.

• TO [UNKNOWN], to have the benefit of forfeiture by gigmills [machines for raising the nap on cloth].

• TO ELIZABETH MATHEWS, for train-oil of blubber [whale oil extracted by boiling blubber].

• TO RICHARD DRAKE, for aqua-composita, aqua-vitae [spirits], vinegar and alegar [malt vinegar].

• TO ROBERT ALEXANDER, for aniseeds.

• TO EDWARD DARCY, for steel.

• TO MICHAEL STANHOPE, for Spanish wool.

• TO VALENTINE HARRIS, to sow six hundred acres of ground with woade.

• TO [UNKNOWN], to take benefit for the statute for gashing of hides.

• TO MR CORNWALLIS, for unlawful games.

• TO HENRY SINGER, touching printing of school books.

• TO ARTHUR BASSANEY, to transport six thousand calf skins.

• TO EDWARD DARCY, to provide, bring, make and utter [sell] cards.

• TO THOMAS MORLEY [the composer], after Byrd and Tallis, to print songs in parts.

• TO SIR JOHN PAKINGTON [an athletic courtier nicknamed Lusty Pakington by the Queen, who rescued him from penury after he lost his fortune] for starch and ashes [used in soap-making].

• TO [UNKNOWN], to make mathematical instruments.

• TO [UNKNOWN], to make saltpetre.

• TO THOMAS WRIGHT and BONHAM NORTON, to print the law-books.

• TO [UNKNOWN], for livers of fishes.

• TO [UNKNOWN], for polldavis [coarse canvas for sails], for fishing.

STURDY ROGUES, BEGGARS AND VAGABONDS

In the sixteenth century the authorities were much concerned by the numbers of able-bodied unemployed roaming the countryside, seeing them as a source of crime and a possible threat to national security. Many reasons for their numbers were put forward then and subsequently: a rise in population from about 3 million in 1550 to 4 million in 1600, enclosures of land and the turning of arable into pasture, price rises, the monasteries no longer being there as a source of charity, great nobles no longer having bands of liveried retainers, Irish emigrants, discharged soldiers. A contemporary pamphlet, *The Caveat for Common Cursetors*, listed the different types of vagabonds and their methods and tricks:

Rufflers sturdy rogues who begged from the strong and robbed the weak

Upright Men vagabond chiefs

Hookers or Anglers stole clothing, etc. through open windows, using a hooked stick

Wild Rogues born on the road of vagabond parents

Priggers of Prancers horse thieves

Palliards created sores on their bodies with corrosive substances so as to elicit sympathy and money

Fraters pretended to be collecting alms for hospitals

Abraham Men pretended to be mad

Whip-Jacks pretended to be shipwrecked sailors

Counterfeit Cranks pretended to be suffering from the falling sickness (epilepsy)

Dommerers pretended to be deaf mutes

Tinkers and Pedlars who used their trade as a cover for thieving

Jarckmen forgers of false licences to beg

Patricoes hedge-priests (illiterate and possibly unordained)

Demanders for Glimmer pretended to have lost their possessions in fires

Bawdy Baskets female vagabonds

Autem Morts women married in a church

Walking Morts unmarried whores

Doxies female companions of vagabonds

Dells young girls not yet broken in by the Upright Men

Kynchen Morts female children

Kynchen Coes male children

For much of the century, the only way of dealing with them was to give them a whipping and then send them back to the parish where they had once lived. Sometimes more severe remedies were tried: 71 beggars were first whipped and then burned through the ear in two months in 1591. But a few years after this the Elizabethan Poor Laws were passed setting up a compulsory poor rate nationwide, with each parish appointing overseers of the poor and setting up workhouses. This system survived until the New Poor Law of 1834.

THE INNS OF COURT AND CHANCERY

These uniquely English institutions, the Inns of Court, owe their position to their total control of admission to the rank of barrister, which carried with it the 'right of audience', the right to be heard, to plead in the law courts. The judges might be expected to control who could plead before them; instead it is the Inns, though of course the judges, promoted from the ranks of barristers, are themselves Inn members. Their monopoly has been somewhat undermined since 1994, when solicitors were also given the right of audience.

The Inns are all located in a small area on the western boundary of the City of London, where they have been since the 14th century. By being equidistant from the City's Guildhall and the Royal Court at Westminster the Inns preserved their independence, yet the lawyers could easily get to the new centralised law courts of the King at Westminster either by boat up the Thames or along the Strand. They began as practical self-help assemblies of lawyers during legal term time, to ensure mutual protection and provide accommodation and communal eating. At some point in the 15th century the Inns started taking unqualified youths and began to teach them law. Many of these were the sons of well-to-do fathers, sent for a few years because of the general educational opportunities rather than to become practising lawyers. After their glory days in the 16th and 17th centuries, the Inns went into a decline in the 18th as fewer lawyers chose to live within their bounds, and non-members were allowed to reside as well as shops to open.

Legal reform in the 19th century, and the expansion of business as a result of the industrial revolution and Britain's general prosperity, meant that the number of lawyers rapidly increased and the Inns flourished once more.

GRAY'S INN is the most northerly, above High Holborn, and in the 16th century was by far the largest and most prestigious Inn, including among its members Queen Elizabeth's ministers William Cecil and Francis Walsingham, as well as Francis Bacon, Philip Sidney and Shakespeare's patron the Earl of Southampton. The 18th and 19th centuries were a period of decline for the Inn, but then its fortunes were revived, particularly by F. E. Smith, Lord Birkenhead, only for it to lose many of its buildings during the Blitz in 1941, including its chapel, hall and library – all now rebuilt.

LINCOLN'S INN is south of High Holborn, between Lincoln's Inn Fields and Chancery Lane. Its Old Hall, the first big building purpose-built for lawyers in London, was finished in 1492 and still stands, as does the Chapel completed in 1623. The Old Hall was made notorious by Dickens setting the opening of *Bleak House* in it: 'London, Michaelmas Term lately over, and the Lord Chancellor sitting in Lincoln's Inn Hall. Implacable November weather . . . Fog everywhere.' Its New Square (begun 1685), Stone Buildings (1780) and New Hall (1843) are all architecturally distinguished.

THE MIDDLE TEMPLE is south of Fleet Street, on land which once belonged to the Knights Templar (see p. 11). Their round church (1160–85 – London's earliest Gothic) serves as chapel for both the Middle and the Inner Temple Inns of Court. Middle Temple Hall is perhaps the most interesting Inn building (1570), both for its double-hammerbeam roof and for the performance of *Twelfth Night* there in 1602.

THE INNER TEMPLE is immediately to the east of Middle Temple Lane, though some of the buildings on that side of the Lane belong to the Middle Temple. Look for the Pegasus (winged horse) badge of the Inner and the lamb-and-flag badge of the Middle Temple to work out ownership. Lord Chief Justices Coke, defender of the independence of the judges from the Crown, and Jeffreys, notorious for the Bloody Assizes at which he presided after Monmouth's Rebellion in 1685, were both members of the Inner Temple. King's Bench Walk is the pick of its architecture.

THE INNS OF CHANCERY had origins as ancient and obscure as those of the Inns of Court, but they never rose to such eminence, because they never had the power to bestow qualifications on lawyers. By the 16th century they were acting as out-stations of the Inns of Court, places where youths were sent for a short period before moving on to one of them. By the 17th century they were being left to the attorneys and solicitors, and now those that have not vanished off the map have severed any connection with the law.

STAPLE INN is on the south side of Holborn by Chancery Lane tube station, its half-timbered facade familiar from the Old Holborn tobacco packet. Behind there is a courtyard and a garden, and it now houses the Institute of Actuaries. It was associated with Gray's Inn.

BARNARD'S INN is also off the south side of Holborn, further east. It began life as Macworth's Inn. By the 19th century Dickens called it 'the dingiest set of buildings ever squeezed together in a rank corner as a club for tom-cats'. From the 1890s to 1959 it was the home of the Mercers School and its tiny hall was rebuilt in the 1930s. Associated with Gray's Inn.

FURNIVAL'S INN, or its site, is now taken up by the Prudential Building on the north side of Holborn. It was associated with Lincoln's Inn until finally dissolved in 1818.

THAVIES INN was just to the south of Holborn Circus and in Dickens' day what remained was a 'narrow street of high houses, like an oblong cistern to hold the fog'. Associated with Lincoln's Inn.

LYON'S INN and NEW INN were on the Aldwych island, where Bush House now is.

THE STRAND INN was where King's College now is and Clement's Inn to the north of St Clement Danes Church. Shakespeare's Justice Shallow, in *Henry IV*, Part Two, was 'once of Clement's Inn; where I think they will talk of mad Shallow yet'.They were associated with the Inner and Middle Temples.

CLIFFORD'S INN, demolished in 1935, lay to the north-east of the junction of Chancery Lane with Fleet Street. Dickens called its garden 'a mouldy little plantation, or cat's preserve', echoing his description of Barnard's Inn.

THE
STUARTS

A NOBLE HOUSEHOLD IN THE 17TH CENTURY

'A catalogue of the household and family of the Right Honourable Richard, Earl of Dorset, in the year of our Lord 1613; and so continued until 1624, at Knole, in Kent.'

AT MY LORD'S TABLE

My Lord	My Lady
My Lady Margaret	My Lady Isabella
Mr Sackville	Mr Frost
John Musgrave	Thomas Garret

AT THE PARLOUR TABLE

Mrs Field	Mrs Willoughby
Mrs Grimsditch	Mrs Stewkly
Mrs Fletcher	Mrs Wood

Mr Dupper Chaplain
Mr Matthew Caldicott my Lord's favourite
Mr Edward Legge Steward
Mr Peter Basket Gentleman of the Horse
Mr Marsh Attendant on my Lady
Mr Woodridge
Mr Cheyney
Mr Duck Page
Mr Josiah Cooper A Frenchman, Page
Mr John Belgrave Page
Mr Billingsley
Mr Graverner Gentleman Usher
Mr Marshall Auditor
Mr Edwards Secretary
Mr Drake Attendant

AT THE CLERKS' TABLE IN THE HALL

Edward Fulks and John Edwards Clerks of the Kitchen
Edward Care Master Cook
William Smith Yeoman of the Buttery
Henry Keble Yeoman of the Pantry
John Mitchell Pastryman
Thomas Vinson Cook
John Elnor Cook
Ralph Hussie Cook

John Avery Usher of the Hall
Robert Elnor Slaughterman
Benjamin Staples Groom of the Great Chamber
Thomas Petley Brewer
William Turner Baker
Francis Steeling Gardener
Richard Wicking Gardener
Thomas Clements Under Brewer
Samuel Vans Caterer
Edward Small Groom of the Wardrobe
Samuel Southern Under Baker
Lowry a French boy

THE NURSERY

| Nurse Carpenter | Widow Ben |
| Jane Sisley | Dorothy Pickenden |

AT THE LONG TABLE IN THE HALL

Robert Care Attendant on my Lord
Mr Gray Attendant likewise
Mr Roger Cook Attendant on my Lady Margaret
Mr Adam Bradford Barber
Mr John Guy Groom of my Lord's Bedchamber
Walter Comestone Attendant on my Lady
Edward Lane Scrivener
Mr Thomas Poor Yeoman of the Wardrobe
Mr Thomas Leonard Master Huntsman
Mr Woodgate Yeoman of the Great Chamber
John Hall Falconer
James Flennel Yeoman of the Granary
Rawlinson Armourer
Moses Shonk Coachman
Anthony Ashly Groom of the Great Horse
Griffin Edwards Groom of my Lady's Horse
Francis Turner Groom of the Great Horse
William Grynes Groom of the Great Horse
Acton Curvett Chief Footman
James Loveall Footman
Sampson Ashley Footman
William Petley Footman
Nicholas James Footman
Paschal Beard Footman
Elias Thomas Footman

Henry Spencer Farrier
Edward Goodsall
John Sant the Steward's Man
Ralph Wise Groom of the Stables
Thomas Petler Under Farrier
John Stephens the Chaplain's Man
John Haite Groom for the Stranger's Horse
Thomas Giles Groom of the Stables
Richard Thomas Groom of the Hall
Christopher Wood Groom of the Pantry
George Owen Huntsman
George Vigeon Huntsman
Thomas Grittan Groom of the Buttery
Solomon the Bird-Catcher
Richard Thornton the Coachman's Man
Richard Pickenden Postillion
William Roberts Groom
The Armourer's Man
Ralph Wise his Servant
John Swift the Porter's Man
John Atkins and Clement Doory Men to carry wood

THE LAUNDRY-MAIDS' TABLE

Mrs Judith Simpton
Mrs Grace Simpton
Penelope Tutty the Lady Margaret's Maid
Anne Mills Dairy-Maid
Prudence Bucher
Anne Howse
Faith Husband
Elinor Thompson
Goodwife Burton
Grace Robinson a Blackamoor
Goodwife Small
William Lewis Porter

KITCHEN AND SCULLERY

Diggory Dyer
Marfidy Snipt
John Watson
Thomas Harman
Thomas Johnson
John Morokoe a Blackamoor

SOME 17TH-CENTURY NAMES

Harbottle Grimston	Bulstrode Whitlocke	Priam Davies
Troilus Turbervile	Praise-God Barbone	Fulke Hunke
Brilliana Harley	Leoline Jenkins	Peregrine Bertie
Faithfull Fortescue	Clowdesley Shovell	Epiphanius Evesham
Endymion Porter	Wallop Brabazon	Freschville Holles
Bussy Basset	Marchamont Needham	Slingsby Bethell
Symonds d'Ewes	Hamon L'Estrange	Hardress Waller
Carnaby Haggerston	Theophilus Jones	Cresswell Levinz
Nathaniel Barnardiston	Shakerly Marmion	Salathiel Lovell
Clipseby Crew	Justinian Isham	Sydnam Poyntz

RANKS IN 17TH-CENTURY SOCIETY

THE PEERAGE Under James I there were 60; by 1688 there were 161.

BARONETS First created in 1611. Hereditary. There were over 400 by 1641 and 800 by 1688. Technically drawn from families which had been entitled to a coat of arms for at least three generations and which owned land to the annual value of at least £1,000. In fact baronetcies were a fund-raising device at this time.

KNIGHTS Not hereditary. Traditionally created by the monarch in return for service, and from those who could afford a charger and a suit of armour, and had a coat of arms. Freely created by James I.

ESQUIRES The heirs and descendants of heirs of the younger sons of peers, the heirs of knights, some office holders such as Justices of the Peace, those whose ancestors had been so called. In 1688 there were reckoned to be 3,000.

GENTLEMEN The younger sons and brothers of esquires and their heirs. In 1688 there were reckoned to be 12,000. In practice, plenty of yeomen and merchants elevated themselves into the ranks of the Gentry and plenty of gentlemen fell out.

GENTRY Confusingly, Baronets, Knights, Esquires, Gentlemen – all those below the rank of Peer – were called, collectively, Gentry. The Gentry were subdivided into:

LESSER OR 'PARISH' GENTRY In Yorkshire this meant an estate of between

50 and 1,000 acres. Might be chosen as High Constables of their hundred or serve on the grand jury at quarter sessions.

MIDDLING GENTRY In Yorkshire, an estate of 1,000 to 5,000 acres.

UPPER GENTRY In Yorkshire, an estate of 5,000 to 20,000 acres.

Middling and Upper Gentry would hold the more elevated positions in local administration: MPs, deputy-lieutenants, leading justices, JPs.

YEOMEN Men possessing freehold land worth 40 shillings a year or more, though in fact many were leaseholders or copyholders, and really it was men who farmed 50 acres or more who were accorded this status. This was the minimum acreage to render one immune to fluctuations from poor harvests. They had incomes ranging from £40 up to £200 a year.

HUSBANDMEN Men farming between 5 and 50 acres. A 30-acre holding should have produced a net profit of £14 or £15 a year, of which £11 went on food for a man, wife and four children.

COTTAGERS AND LABOURERS Though they might hold a few acres, they also had to work for wages for others. Perhaps two-thirds of labourers held only their cottages and garden plots. A daily wage was about one shilling, and the wolf was never far from the door.

A Stuart Knight, Sir Thomas Urquhart

BOILED TEATS AND SEAGULLS:
TWO 17TH-CENTURY BANQUET MENUS

These banquets were held at Knole in Kent, home of the Earls of Dorset. Redeeve or reddeeve maybe comes from the Latin *redivivus*, meaning come to life again.

1	Rice Pottage	18	Crabs
2	Barley broth	19	Tench pie
3	Buttered pickrell [young pike]	20	Venison pasty of a Doe
4	Buttered and burned eggs	21	Sawns [swans] (2)
5	Boiled teats	22	Herons (3)
6	Roast tongues	23	Cold lamb
7	Bream	24	Custard
8	Perches	25	Venison, boiled
9	Chine of Veal roast	26	Potatoes, stewed
10	Hash of mutton with anchovies	27	Gr. salad
11	Gr. Pike	28	Redeeve pie, hot
12	Fish chuits [?cheeks]	29	Almond pudding
13	Roast venison, in blood	30	Made dishes
14	Capons (2)	31	Boiled salad
15	Wild ducks (3)	32	Pig, whole
16	Salmon whole, hot	33	Rabbits
17	Tenches, boiled		

ANOTHER MENU

1	Jelly of Tench, Jelly of Hartshorn [shavings of red deer horn]	17	Seagulls
2	White Gingerbread	18	Ham of bacon
3	Puits [peewits]	19	Sturgeon
4	Curlew pie	20	Lark pie
5	Ruffes	21	Lobster pie
6	Fried perches	22	Crayfishes (3 doz.)
7	Fried Eels	23	Dried tongues
8	Skirret pie [water-parsnip]	24	Anchovies
9	Larks (3 doz.)	25	Hartechocks [artichokes]
10	Plovers (12)	26	Peas
11	Teals (12)	27	Fool
12	Fried Pickrell	28	Second porridge
13	Fried tench	29	Reddeeve pie
14	Salmon soused	30	Cherry tart
15	Soused eel	31	Laid tart
16	Escanechea	32	Carps (2)
		33	Polony [Polish sausage]

At the top of the first menu there are the following instructions: 'To perfume the room often in the meal with orange flower water upon a hot pan. To have fresh bowls in every corner and flowers tied upon them, and sweet briar, stock, gilly-flowers, pinks, wallflowers and any other sweet flowers in glasses and pots in every window and chimney.'

FATAL DISEASES AND OTHER CAUSES OF DEATH IN LONDON, 1629–1835

The columns of figures are the yearly average number of deaths attributed to the diseases, etc. listed in the left-hand column during the period indicated at the top of each of the columns of figures.

	7 Years 1629–35	20 Years 1660–79	30 Years 1728–57	10 Years 1771–80	5 Years 1831–35
Abortives and still-born		26.8	23.0		
Chrisomes	247.1	36.1	—	—	—
Overlaid	1.1	2.8	—	0.2	—
Convulsions	22.2	77.8	277.0	271.0	92.6
Worms	2.7	1.5	0.5	0.3	0.2
Teething	49.7	54.0	50.0	36.0	14.1
Inflammation of the brain	—	—	—	—	5.7
Mold-shot head, dropsy on the brain	—	0.4	4.0	1.0	33.2
Rickets	1.0	17.6	2.0	0.1	—
Livergrown	8.5	0.9	0.2	0.05	—
Canker, thrush	3.3	3.4	4.3	3.8	4.4
Croup	—	—	—	—	5.8
Chin-cough	—	1.2	5.2	17.3	39.5
The above infantile diseases	336.2	195.7	343.2	329.75	195.3
Small-pox	37.8	50.9	80.0	100.3	26.9
Measles	3.3	5.8	7.0	9.5	27.0
Swine-pox, chicken-pox, rash	0.6	0.1	1.01	0.1	—
St. Anthony's Fire, or erysipelas	—	0.06	0.1	0.1	2.9

	7 Years 1629–35	20 Years 1660–79	30 Years 1728–57	10 Years 1771–80	5 Years 1831–35
Fever, Scarlet	—	—	—	—	16.7
Fever	127.1	95.9	148.3	124.1	33.8
intermittent	—	—	—	—	0.8
spotted	9.0	11.1	—	—	—
Plague	25.0	161.7	—	—	—
Griping of guts, colic, twisting, wind	2.2	102.5	9.0	2.3	0.4
Bloody flux, flux	42.5	6.7	1.4	1.0	—
Cholera mobus or surfeit...	12.6	18.5	0.1	0.5	42.3
Vomiting and looseness, diarrhoea	0.3	1.6	0.6	0.3	1.4
Stopping of the stomach.....	0.3	12.6	5.0	—	—
Constipation	—	—	—	—	1.0
Rupture	0.6	1.3	0.7	0.5	1.2
Quinsey, sore throat	0.8	1.5	0.7	1.0	1.5
Cough and cold	5.1	—	—	0.2	—
Pleurisy	2.8	0.7	2.0	1.0	12.1
Influenza	—	—	—	—	1.2
Inflammation	—	—	2.0	6.2	96.0
of bowels, stomach	—	—	—	—	15.2
Indigestion	—	—	—	—	0.3
Disease of the heart	—	—	—	—	5.4
Asthma and Tissick	—	—	21.0	17.1	42.4
Consumption	204.1	153.4	170.0	224.3	177.2
King's Evil	2.7	2.4	1.0	1.0	0.9
Fistula	2.6	2.1	0.5	0.2	0.1
Stricture	—	—	—	—	0.7
French pox	1.5	3.0	3.0	3.1	0.2
Cancer	—	—	2.0	3.4	4.4
Sores, ulcers	2.4	2.6	1.0	0.8	—
Mortification	—	v.fistula	9.0	9.9	10.6
Abscess, imposthume	7.3	5.0	1.0	0.2	6.6
Tumour	—	—	—	0.1	1.2
Scald head, itch, leprosy....	—	—	0.4	0.2	—
Scurvy	0.4	2.6	0.1	0.2	—
Gravel, stone, strangury.....	5.0	3.0	1.0	1.9	0.9

	1629–35	1660–79	1728–57	1771–80	1831–35
Gout, sciatica	0.3	0.6	2.0	3.1	3.1
Rheumatism	—	—	—	—	1.7
Jaundice	6.5	3.7	5.0	5.8	2.1
Liver disease	—	—	—	—	12.8
Diabetes	—	—	0.06	0.05	0.3
Dropsy	29.7	42.6	41.0	45.1	37.6
on the chest	—	—	—	—	4.0
Bleeding piles	0.4	0.1	0.2	0.4	2.0
Apoplexy	2.5	3.7	9.0	11.1	18.5
suddenly	6.7	—	—	—	—
Palsy, lethargy	2.8	2.0	2.3	3.7	8.6
Spleen and vapours	—	0.3	0.05	—	—
Green sickness	—	—	0.002	—	—
Rising of the lights and mother	8.3	9.1	0.5	0.02	—
Grief	1.7	0.6	0.4	0.2	—
Fright	0.03	0.1	—	—	—
Falling sickness	0.6	0.06	0.01	—	1.5
Jawfallen	1.1	0.02	—	—	0.2
Spasm	—	—	—	—	2.9
Blasted, planet-struck	0.8	0.1	—	—	—
Calenture, megrims	0.4	0.2	—	—	—
Headache	—	—	0.03	0.05	—
Lunacy	0.5	0.4	3.0	2.7	7.6
Hydrophobia	—	—	—	0.03	0.2
Various	0.4	0.8	—	0.03	—
Old age, bedridden	74.1	47.4	78.0	64.7	111.5
Unknown causes	—	—	—	—	27.4
Found dead	1.9	0.4	—	0.3	0.3
Visitation of God	—	—	—	—	1.8
Starved	—	0.04	—	0.2	0.01
Killed of drinking to excess	—	—	—	0.5	0.4
Suicide	0.7	0.7	—	1.6	2.2
Drowned	3.8	3.3	—	5.8	5.0
Smothered	0.6	0.1	—	0.3	0.04
Burned	0.6	0.4	—	0.6	—
Poisoned	0.03	0.1	—	0.06	0.3
Killed	5.4	2.8	—	3.1	—
Accidents	—	—	—	0.3	7.4
Murdered	0.3	0.6	—	0.3	0.17
Executed	1.6	0.8	—	1.1	0.16
Childbed & miscarriage	16.1	12.2	8.0	9.4	13.4

'The names of diseases, although derived generally from some very striking feature in the case, are not infrequently vague and obsolete.' A chrisom was a baby that died within a month of birth. The mold-shot head was a chronic form of water on the brain (hydrocephalus). Livergrown was swelling of the abdomen, the liver and the spleen. Scarlet Fever was only made a separate item in 1831. Griping, twisting of the guts, bloody flux and plague in the guts were 'the homely Saxon synonyms of dysentery'. Surfeit (dysentery) epidemics in August were attributed to eating too much fruit. King's evil was scrofula, tuberculosis, especially of the lymph glands. Diseases of childbed, often accompanied by hysterical symptoms, were evidently reported under the title of rising of the lights.

CHARLES II'S BASTARDS

BY MARGARET CARTERET OF JERSEY – James, a Jesuit (1646–67?)

BY LUCY WALTER (d. 1658) – James Scott, Duke of Monmouth, born 1649. He married Anne Scott, Countess of Buccleuch in her own right, taking her surname. He was executed after the failure of his rising against his Catholic uncle, James II, in 1685. He always claimed that his parents had been married and in the nineteenth century the then Duke of Buccleuch is said to have thrown their marriage lines, preserved by his family, on the fire because he did not wish them ever to become an embarrassment to Queen Victoria.

BY ELIZABETH KILLIGREW, LATER LADY SHANNON – Charlotte FitzRoy (1650–84) who married firstly James Howard, Earl of Suffolk, and secondly William Paston, Earl of Yarmouth.

BY KATHERINE PEGGE – Charles FitzCharles, Earl of Plymouth (1657–80). A daughter, Katherine, became a nun at Dunkirk.

BY BARBARA CASTLEMAINE (1641–1709), daughter of William Villiers, Lord Grandison who was a nephew of James I's and Charles I's favourite, the Duke of Buckingham. She married Roger Palmer, Earl of Castlemaine, and later became Duchess of Cleveland in her own right -
1) Anne FitzRoy (1661–1722) who married Thomas Lennard, Earl of Sussex.
2) Charles FitzRoy (1662–1730) Duke of Southampton and Cleveland
3) Henry FitzRoy (1663–1690) Duke of Grafton
4) Charlotte FitzRoy (1663–1717) who married Edward Henry Lee, Earl of Lichfield
5) George FitzRoy (1665–1716) Duke of Northumberland
6) Barbara (1672–1737) Prioress of the Hotel Dieu, Pontoise. Her mother

claimed Charles was her father but it is more probable that she was the daughter of John Churchill, 1st Duke of Marlborough. Among Lady Castlemaine's other lovers were the Earl of Chesterfield, Ralph Montagu, English ambassador to France, and Jacob Hall the rope-dancer.

BY NELL GWYNNE, an actress – Charles Beauclerk (1670–1726) Duke of St Albans. Also James Beauclerk who died aged nine in 1680.

BY LOUISE DE KÉROUAILLE (1649–1734), Duchess of Portsmouth in her own right – Charles Lennox (1672–1723) Duke of Richmond.

BY MOLL DAVIES, an actress – Mary Tudor (1673–1726). She married firstly Edward Radcliffe, 2nd Earl of Derwentwater, secondly Henry Graham of Levens and thirdly James Rooke. Her son James, 3rd Earl of Derwentwater, was beheaded in 1716 for his part in the 1715 Jacobite rising. His brother Charles, imprisoned and awaiting trial at Newgate for the same offence, escaped with 13 others, only to be beheaded in 1746 after being implicated in the 1745 Jacobite rising.

The present Dukes of Buccleuch, Grafton, St Albans and Richmond are all descended from these liaisons.

When the mob jostled Nell Gwynne's coach, mistaking it for that of the unpopular Catholic Louise de Kérouaille, Nell leant out and said, 'Pray, good people, be civil; I am the Protestant whore.'

The Duchess of Portsmouth (Louise de Kérouaille), Lady Dorchester and Lady Orkney had been mistresses to Charles II, James II and William III respectively. When old ladies they went to George I's Court where Lady Dorchester said, 'God! Who would have thought we three whores should have met here!'

Charles II did not hold the record for the number of bastards fathered by an English king. This is thought to belong to Henry I, who had twenty or possibly twenty-two, and six mistresses.

'It may be said that his inclinations to love were the effects of health, and a good constitution, with as little mixture of the seraphick part as any man had. And though from that foundation men often raise their passions, I am apt to think his stayed as much as any man's ever did in the lower region . . . After he was restored . . . it was resolved generally by others, whom he should have in his arms, as well as whom he should have in his Councils. Of a man who was capable of choosing, he chose as seldom as any man that ever lived.'

George Savile, Marquess of Halifax (1633–95), on Charles II

THE CRIES OF LONDON

Pedlars and street sellers advertised what they had to offer, whether goods or services, by shouting their wares as they walked by. In 1687 the artist Marcellus Laroon's series of prints of such men and women were published under the title *Habits and Cryes of the City of London Drawne after the Life*, and each print had the relevant cry printed at its foot.

A Bed Matt or a Door Matt
A Merry New Song
Any Card matches or Savealls
Any Kitchin Stuffe have you maids
Any work for John Cooper
Buy a fine Table Basket
Buy a Fork or Fire Shovel
Buy a Rabbet a Rabbet
Buy a new Almanack
Buy any Wax or Wafers
Buy my Dish of great Eeles
Buy my Dutch Biskets
Buy my Four Ropes of Hard Onyons
Colly Molly Puffe
Crab Crab any Crab
Delicate Cowcumbers to pickle
Fair Lemons and Oranges
Four for six pence Mackrell
Knives Combs or Inkhornes

Four paire for a Shilling Holland Socks
Any Bakeing Peares
Knives or Cisers to Grinde
Lilly white Vinegar 3 pence a quart
Londons Gazette here
Long Threed Laces Long and Strong
New River Water
Old Chaires to mend
Old Satten Old Taffety or Velvet
Old Shooes for Some Broomes
Pretty Maids Pretty Pins Pretty Women
Remember the Poor Prisoners
Ripe Speragas
Ripe Strawberryes
Six pence a pound fair Cherryes
Twelve Pence a Peck Oysters
Fine Writeing Inke
Hott Bak'd Wardens Hott
[pies made of Warden pears]

Herb Wife

Rabbit Man

Mouse Trap Seller

THE GROWTH OF TOWNS

The three tables below show how English towns grew over three centuries, and the changes in their rankings based on their population figures. London was always a law unto itself. In 1600 it had 250,000 inhabitants; in 1650, 400,000; in 1700, 575,000; in 1750, 675,000; and in 1851, 2,363,000. By 1760 it was the greatest city in the world, bar Constantinople, but only in 1790 did its death rate drop below its birth rate.

By 1750 1.5 million, 25 per cent, of England's inhabitants lived in towns with a population of 2,500 or more. In 1650 the proportion had been half this. By 1851 more than half England's inhabitants were town dwellers. Birmingham does not feature on the 1670 table because its population then was only 4,400. In 1851 Dublin had 405,000, Glasgow 375,000, Edinburgh 202,000, and Belfast 103,000.

The 25 leading Provincial Towns c.1670		The 25 leading Provincial Towns c.1750		The 25 leading Provincial Towns c.1851	
Norwich	21,000	Bristol	50,000	Liverpool	395,000
Bristol	18,000	Norwich	36,000	Manchester	338,000
Exeter	12,500	Newcastle	29,000	Birmingham	265,000
Newcastle	11,800	Birmingham	23,700	Leeds	172,000
York	10,500	Liverpool	22,000	Bristol	137,000
Gt Yarmouth	9,500	Manchester	18,000	Sheffield	135,000
Colchester	9,500	Exeter	16,000	Bradford	104,000
Worcester	8,500	Plymouth	15,000	Plymouth	90,000
Ipswich	7,500	Leeds	13,000	Newcastle	88,000
Canterbury	7,500	Chester	13,000	Salford	85,000
Chester	7,500	Coventry	12,500	Hull	85,000
Plymouth	7,500	Ipswich	12,100	Portsmouth	72,000
Oxford	7,500	Sheffield	12,000	Preston	70,000
Cambridge	7,300	Nottingham	12,000	Norwich	68,000
Shrewsbury	7,100	Hull	11,500	Brighton	66,000
Salisbury	6,700	York	11,400	Stoke-on-	
Coventry	6,500	Worcester	10,300	Trent	66,000
Hull	6,300	Gt Yarmouth	10,000	Sunderland	64,000
Bury St.		Sunderland	10,000	Bolton	61,000
Edmunds	5,500	Portsmouth	10,000	Leicester	61,000
Manchester	5,500	Bath	9,000	Nottingham	57,000
Nottingham	5,500	King's Lynn	9,000	Stockport	54,000
Leicester	5,000	Canterbury	8,600	Bath	54,000
Hereford	5,000	Colchester	8,500	Oldham	52,000
Tiverton	5,000	Oxford	8,200	Wolverh'ton	50,000
Gloucester	4,700			Blackburn	47,000

THE
LONG 18TH CENTURY

ROADS AND COACHES

'I saw an ancient lady, and a lady of very good quality, I assure you, drawn to church in her coach with six oxen; nor was it done in frolic or humour, but mere necessity, the way being so stiff and deep, that no horses could go in it.'

Daniel Defoe, A Tour through the Whole Island of Great Britain, *1724–27. This incident took place near Lewes in Sussex.*

These were the sorts of conditions with which travellers had to contend until the network of turnpike roads was extended in the later 18th century. The TURNPIKES OR TOLL BARS were the barriers across roads at which travellers paid their tolls, which were then spent on their building and upkeep. The first turnpike was established on a stretch of the GREAT NORTH ROAD (the A1) in 1663. In the earlier 1700s about eight toll roads a year were begun but from 1751 to 1772 this number went up to forty a year, and the country was quickly criss-crossed. The surveyors of the turnpike trusts developed a roadbuilding method which relied on firm foundations and a convex surface from which water could drain off into ditches on either side. (JOHN MCADAM, one of the most renowned, in fact did not bother with foundations.) The surface was of stones, none being more than one square inch in surface area, since that was the amount of a wheel rim in contact with them.

The improvement in the road system allowed STAGE COACHES to proliferate. In 1680 there were services to 88 towns from London; by 1715 there were services to 216. In 1740 there was a single daily coach to Birmingham; by 1783 there were thirty. Then from 1784 the system of MAIL COACHES was established, carrying passengers, letters and packets, under the direction of John Palmer, a theatre owner of Bath. The Post Office fixed the timetables and provided armed guards. The coaches were exempt from tolls and went 8 m.p.h. when introduced, but faster later. They were pulled by six horses which were changed every ten miles and had a working life of only three years. In 1740 it took 40 hours to travel the 114 miles from London to Bristol. By 1812 the time was down to about 12 hours. But the fares were not cheap: between about 1½d and 2½d a mile to travel inside.

In 1804 coach suspension systems were transformed by Obadiah Elliott's invention, the ELLIPTICAL METAL SPRING. Before, coach bodies had hung, swaying sickeningly, from leather straps. Elliptical springs allowed double the number of passengers to be carried in much greater comfort.

The names adopted for mail coaches were splendidly evocative of speed and other desirable qualities: TELEGRAPHS, HIGHFLIERS, BALLOON COACHES, DEFIANCES, HOPES, PERSEVERANCES, REGULATORS, GOOD INTENTS.

FOOTPADS AND HIGHWAYMEN

Henry Fielding the novelist and his blind half-brother Sir John Fielding were both Westminster magistrates in the middle of the 18th century, when they pioneered the employment of 'thief-takers', the precursors of the later Bow Street Runners, so-called after the location of the magistrates' court. In a letter dated 28 June 1764, Sir John wrote to the Secretary to the Treasury urging 'the amazing importance of police to Government', in spite of the expense. As an appendix to his letter he listed the crimes committed round London in the previous week.

1. Christopher Pratt, driver of Mr Stanton's waggon of Market Harborough with the Bedford and Huntingdon waggoners robbed on Finchley Common on Friday night by two footpads, who beat and wounded them much.

2. Francis Walker, master coachman, of Nag's Head Yard, Oxford Road, drives No. 325, robbed on Tuesday night by two or three footpads near Paddington, of his own watch and money and two ladies of their purses.

3. Mr Taylor of King Street, Golden Square, brewer, in company with another gentleman, robbed the same night near Gunnersbury House, by a single highwayman.

4. The Honourable Mrs Grey, robbed the same night near Sion House, by a highwayman.

5. Mr Kearr, whipmaker of the Mews, with three other gentlemen in post-chaises, all robbed the same night near Turnham Green, by a highwayman.

6. Mr Jackson, of Great Queen Street, robbed in one of the Hampstead stages, near Kentish Town, by a single highwayman, on Monday night.

7. The Bath and Bristol coaches on Hounslow Heath, Tuesday night.

8. Mr Rosser, near Islington, last night, of his gold watch, by two footpads.

He also added that the previous night he had sent out a four-man patrol 'into the fields near Tyburn and Tottenham Court Roads, to search the ditches where footpads have lately infested...Before they got out of the coach which carried them to the spot, they narrowly escaped being murdered by three footpads who, without giving them the least notice, fired two pistols immediately into the coach, but thank God without effect; two of them were afterwards taken, though not before one of them was dangerously wounded.'

STUDIES IN 18TH-CENTURY OXFORD

Edward Gibbon said of his fourteen months at Magdalen College in the 1750s that they were 'the most idle and unprofitable of my whole life . . .The Tutor and pupil lived in the same college as strangers to each other.' Earlier in the century Benjamin Marshall was lucky enough to find himself under a conscientious tutor, and he was able to send his former headmaster a most impressive timetable of his average day.

	Rise before dawn.
6 a.m.	Public Latin prayers.
	Breakfast.
	A walk with my friends, half an hour.
	Study of the Minor Prophets.
	Study of the poem of Tograeus.
9 a.m.	Study of Philosophy.
10 a.m.	To my Tutor, Mr Pelling, who expounds some portion of Philosophy to me and my friends.
11 a.m.	Luncheon.
	With my friends to coffee-house, where we discuss public affairs.
1 p.m.	Study of the Koran.
4 p.m.	Study of Aristotle's Rhetoric.
6 p.m.	Dinner.
	Read Horace's Odes or Martial's epigrams, or mix with my friends in a sociable way.
9 p.m.	Public Latin prayers. In the morning we pray for success upon our doings, and in the evening we return thanks for such success as has been secured.

GOOD BEHAVIOUR AT BATH

In 1705 RICHARD NASH, an unsuccessful gambler and bookmaker, arrived at Bath. The confidence of the local tradespeople had recently been badly shaken by an attack from a disgruntled doctor on the efficacy of the town's thermal springs, and when Nash undertook to restore Bath's position if they placed the superintendence of its public amusements in his hands, they accepted. His first step as MASTER OF CEREMONIES was to draw up a code of conduct and post it in the PUMP ROOM:

1. That a visit of ceremony at first coming, and another at going away, are all that can be expected or desired by ladies of quality and fashion, except impertinents.
2. That ladies coming to the ball appoint a time for their footmen coming to wait on them home, to prevent disturbance and inconveniences to themselves and others.
3. That gentlemen of fashion, never appearing in the morning before the ladies in gowns and caps, shew breeding and respect.
4. That no person take it ill that any one goes to another's play or breakfast, and not theirs – except captious by nature.
5. That no gentleman gives his ticket for the balls to any but gentlewomen.
NB. Unless he has none of his acquaintance.
6. That gentlemen crowding before the ladies at the ball shew ill-manners, and that none do so for the future – except such as respect nobody but themselves.
7. That no gentleman or lady takes it ill that another dances before them – except such as have no pretence to dance at all.
8. That the elder ladies and children be content with a second bench at the ball, as being past or not come to perfection.
9. That the younger ladies take notice how many eyes observe them.
10. That all whisperers of lies and scandal be taken for their authors.
11. That all repeaters of such lies and scandal be shunn'd by all company – except such as have been guilty of the same crime.
NB. Several men of no character, old women and young ones of questioned reputation, are great authors of lies in these places, being of the sect of levellers.

BEAU NASH'S next step was to persuade the ladies visiting Bath to give up the fashion for wearing white aprons, which he regarded as a rustic affectation. When the Duchess of Queensberry appeared in one, he snatched it off her, yet she quietly submitted. Then he turned his attention to the young country squires, getting them to abandon their boots in favour of shoes and stockings. No one was to wear a sword, either. The ASSEMBLY ROOMS were built under his direction, but perhaps Nash's greatest innovation was what the novelist Tobias Smollett called 'the general mixture of all degrees assembled in our public rooms, without distinction of rank or fortune... Yesterday morning, at the Pump

Room, I saw a broken-winded Wapping landlady squeeze through a circle of peers, to salute her brandy merchant ... and a paralytic attorney of Shoe Lane, in shuffling up to the bar, kicked the shins of the Chancellor of England.' All were to minuet in strict rotation, rather than in order of rank. In spite of this, by the middle of the century Bath's position as the most fashionable resort was unassailable. In 1765 visitors there included: 3 princes, 4 dukes, 4 duchesses, 1 marquess, 2 marchionesses, 24 earls, 22 countesses, 14 viscounts, 43 viscountesses, 12 barons, 12 baronesses and 6 bishops.

THE COST OF LIVING IN LONDON IN 1767

In that year there was published *Considerations on the Expediency of Raising, at this Time of General Dearth, the Wages of Servants that are not Domestic, particularly Clerks in Public Office:*

That Fifty Pounds a Year is abundantly sufficient for the subsistence of clerks in public offices ... is as absurd and impudent [a statement] as it is false and malignant. I have made the following estimate [to show so].

	£	s	d
BREAKFAST	0	0	2
Bread and cheese, and small beer, from the chandler's shop.			
DINNER	0	0	7
Chuck-beef, or scrag of mutton, or sheeps' trotters, or pig's ear soused; cabbage or potatoes, or parsnips; bread, and small beer, with half a pint of porter.			
SUPPER	0	0	3
Bread and cheese, with radishes or cucumbers, or onions.			
Small beer, and half a pint of porter	0	0	1½
	0	1	1½
Multiplied by 7	0	7	10½
AN ADDITIONAL REPAST ON SUNDAY	0	0	4
	0	8	2½

	£	s	d
Lodging in a ready-furnished room	0	2	6
Washing	0	0	10
Shaving and combing a wig twice	0	0	6
Pleasures. Saturday-night's club, one tankard of porter	0	0	3½
	0	12	4
Multiplied by 52	32	1	4
Apparel, coals, candles	16	4	9
Soap, blacking, pepper, vinegar and salt	0	10	0
Church expense	0	10	0
(if he is not an avowed enemy of the Christian Faith)			
The lady's maid at Christmas	0	1	0
Balance Saved	0	12	9
TOTAL	50	0	0

…For the common Entertainments of Life, such as almost all people partake of, I have left him wholly dependent upon the bounty of others; not allowing him, at his own cost, one night at Sadlers-Wells, one drop of wine or punch, one dish of tea or coffee, one pennyworth of fruit, one pipe of tobacco, or one pinch of snuff; and the ten shillings church expences include the sum-total of his yearly bounty to the poor. I have driven him to the dirtiest and meanest parts of town, to seek for a cheap lodging; I have cloathed him in the plainest and coarsest manner; I have scarcely allowed him to be clean enough for the place of his stated appearance; I have fed him with the refuse of the market … and I have granted him no indulgence but his Saturday night's club of three-pence half-penny, that he may forget for a few hours the toils and cares of the past week …

HIGHLAND CLANS

The map indicates the approximate locations of the Highland clans in the Jacobite period. Any such map must be treated with care because clan society was much more fluid than it would seem to indicate. The determining element of a clan was not so much a geographical location or the bearing of a surname, as allegiance to a particular chief. Few clans had a neat block of territory, and clan maps tend to indicate merely where a particular surname predominated. Certainly not all the members of a clan were related by blood, even if they bore the clan surname.

While the Highlands were no more violent than the rest of Scotland or the Borders in the 15th and 16th centuries, clan wars did continue there well into the 17th. However, these had died down by the time of the first Jacobite rebellion in 1715, and in fact the OLD PRETENDER received more support from the North-East Lowlands than from the Highlands. Up to 1745 Highland society was more tranquil than for many centuries, and its real problem was poverty, 'the death of cattle and scarcity of victuale'.

There were many Highlanders who took part in the '45, the second Jacobite rebellion, but not all fought for BONNIE PRINCE CHARLIE; there were plenty who did not 'come out' or were on the Hanoverian side, principally the Campbells.

THE HIGHLANDERS WHO FOUGHT AT CULLODEN
(in order from the right of the line)

Athollmen – Robertsons of Struan, Menzies of Shian, Murrays

Camerons of Lochaber

Stewarts of Appin, with some MacLarens, McColls, Carmichaels, Livingstones and MacLeays

Frasers

Clan Chattan – Macintoshes, MacGillivrays, MacBeans

Farquharsons of Monaltrie and Balmoral

MacLachlans, MacLeans and Chisholms

Macdonalds/Macdonells – Clanranald, Keppoch, Glengarry (including some MacLeods and Grants), Glencoe, Barisdale, Kinloch Moidart, Morar

[The Macphersons and MacGregors missed the battle.]

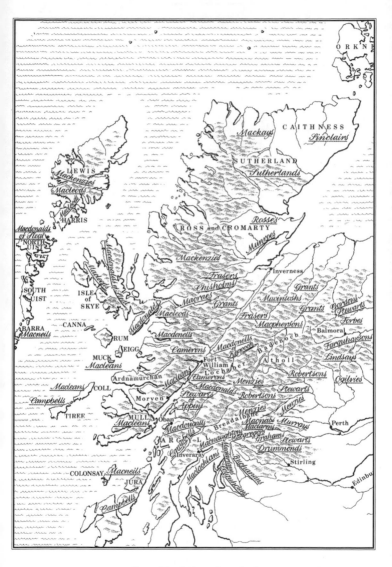

The Highland Clans of Scotland

WATERWAYS

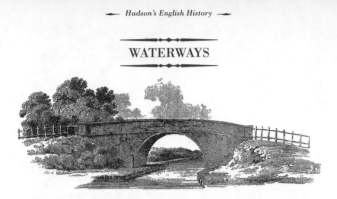

The first stage towards a water transport network in Britain was a series of improvements to rivers. In 1694 work began on making the MERSEY navigable up to Warrington and gradually, by the building of locks, by dredging and by excavating new 'cuts', it and other rivers were made usable. By the 1730s there were few stretches of river left that could be treated in this way, but the financial incentives for transporting goods, and coal in particular, by water remained. The cost of a load of coal was doubled if it had to travel ten miles by road from the pithead. A packhorse could carry two or three hundredweight, but a horse could tow thirty tons on a river, and fifty tons on the still waters of a canal. THE DUKE OF BRIDGEWATER'S CANAL, from his coalpits at Worsley into Manchester, was completed in 1761, resulting in the halving of the cost of coal in the town. Under the stimulus of its example canal schemes were started in every direction. In 1772, for example, the STAFFORDSHIRE AND WORCESTERSHIRE CANAL linked the Severn with the Mersey, while the RUNCORN CANAL linked the Worsley canal with the sea. In 1777 the GRAND TRUNK CANAL linked the Severn, the Trent and the Mersey, so joining the North Sea, the Irish Sea and the Bristol Channel. In the 1790s new canals in South Wales enabled supplies of coal and of iron ore to be brought together. In 1805 the GRAND JUNCTION CANAL linked the Midlands with London.

'The capital improvement wrought since I was here before is the canal to Oxford, Coventry, Wolverhampton, etc.; the port, as it may be called, or double canal head in the town crowded with coal barges is a noble spectacle, with that prodigious animation, which the immense trade of this place alone could give. I looked around me with amazement at the change effected in twelve years; so great that this place may now probably be reckoned with justice, the first manufacturing town in the world. From this port and these quays you may now go by water to Hull, Liverpool, Bristol, Oxford and London. The cut was opened through the coal mines to Wolverhampton in 1769; in 1783, into the new mines of Wednesbury, and to the junction with the Coventry canal... Coals, before these canals were made, were 6*d* per cwt at Birmingham, now 4 ½*d*.' – *Arthur Young on Birmingham, from his* Tour in England and Wales, *1791.*

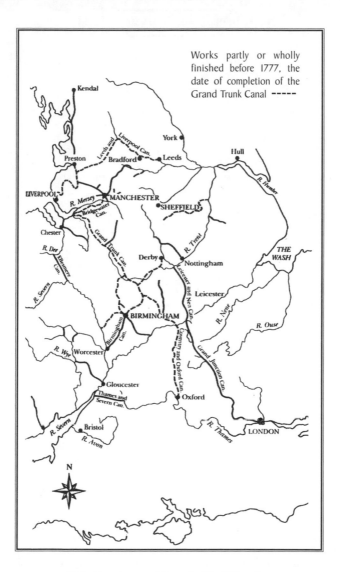

Works partly or wholly finished before 1777, the date of completion of the Grand Trunk Canal -----

Navigable waterways at the end of the 18th century

THE 18TH-CENTURY GIN SCARE

The taste for gin was one of the imports from Holland that arrived in the train of King William after 1688, like tulips and blue-and-white Delft earthenware. Flavour was given to the spirit by adding juniper berries, in Dutch called genever, and shortened in English to gin. In 1700 the average adult in England drank about a third of a gallon of cheap spirits a year; in 1720, two-thirds of a gallon; in 1729, 1.3 gallons; in 1743, 2.2 gallons. The reasons for the rise in consumption seem to have been:

• Improved yields from agriculture joined to a slowing-down in the growth of population, leading to higher wages and cheaper food, in turn leading to surplus wages, which could be spent on gin.

• Landowners happy to sell their surplus grain to the distillers, and ensuring protectionist acts were passed by Parliament to keep out foreign spirits. The government rapidly coming to depend on the duty on gin.

• This being the mass market's first encounter with spirits and rapid intoxication, it led to impaired judgement and so to over-indulgence.

• Gin drinking was a particularly London phenomenon. The population of London increasing greatly during this period, turning to gin as an escape from the poverty, overcrowding and the new pressures of urban immigrant life.

Once the 'gin craze' was identified as such, pressure mounted for action to be taken to curb consumption. This led to eight separate 'gin acts' being passed by parliament between 1729 and 1751.

Gin acquired many aliases and its impact was much greater because it came on the back of a large consumption of strong beer, also with colourful names.

NAMES FOR GIN { Sangree, Tow-Row, Cuckold's Comfort, Bob, Makeshift, Ladies' Delight, The Baulk, King Theodore of Corsica

NAMES FOR STONG BEER { Ram-Jam, Stingo, Hock-Me-Jockey, Staggering Bob, Knock-Me-Down, Strike-Me-Dead

Consumption started to fall from the mid-1740s thanks to a combination of increased duty and the driving-down of wages from population growth and bad harvests, leaving no surplus to spend on gin. In 1752 consumption was back down to 1.2 gallons and in 1757 to less than two-thirds of a gallon.

DIET IN A TYPICAL ENGLISH WORKHOUSE

The Bill of Fare at the 'House of Industry' at Heckingham in Norfolk was published in 1797, in the days of the Old Poor Law, and gave 250 ounces of solid food each week to an adult male pauper.

	BREAKFAST	DINNER	SUPPER
SUN	Bread and cheese, and butter, or treacle	Dumplins, butcher's meat, and bread	Bread and cheese, or butter
MON	The same as Sunday	Broth and bread	Ditto
TUE	Milk and water gruel, and bread	Baked suet puddings	Ditto
WED	The same as Sunday	Dumplins & milk broth; or milk and water gruel	Ditto
THU	The same as Tuesday	The same as Sunday	Ditto
FRI	The same as Sunday	The same as Monday	Ditto
SAT	The same as Tuesday	Bread and cheese, or butter	Ditto

'The men are, each, allowed a pint of beer at every meal, except when they have broth, or gruel. Women, with children at the breast, have the same allowance. Others have two-thirds of a pint.'

After the New Poor Law was passed in 1834, Heckingham's 'General Dietary', as it was now called, only provided 178 ounces each week. The aim now was that workhouses be 'as repulsive as is consistent with humanity'.

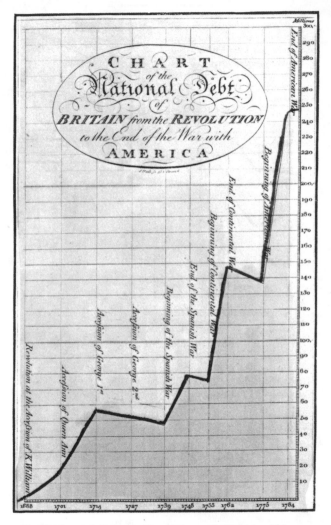

CHART
of the
National Debt
of
BRITAIN from the REVOLUTION
to the End of the War with
AMERICA

Millions
300.

290

280

270

260

250

240

230

220

210

200,

190

180

170

160

150

140

130

120

110

100,

90

80

70

60

50

40

30

20

10

End of American War

Beginning of American War

End of Continental War

Beginning of Continental War

End of the Spanish War

Beginning of the Spanish War

Accession of George 2nd

Accession of George 1st

Accession of Queen Ann

Revolution at the Accession of K. William

1688   1701   1714   1727   1739   1748   1755   1762   1775   1784

The Divisions at the Bottom are Years, & those on the Right hand Money.

TAX AND THE NATIONAL DEBT

'In this world nothing can be said to be certain, except death and taxes.'
Benjamin Franklin

'To tax and to please, no more than to love and to be wise, is not given to men.'
Edmund Burke

In the Middle Ages irregularly levied direct taxes took the form of FIFTEENTHS and TENTHS, fractions of the value of moveable property and income – a fifteenth in the Shires and a tenth in the Boroughs. Customs, called TUNNAGE AND POUNDAGE, were indirect taxes on imported and exported goods, the most significant being the levy of one mark (six shillings and eight pence) on each sack of wool exported. This was later transferred to cloth exports. During the Civil War John Pym, the Parliamentarian leader, introduced EXCISE, duties on goods produced and consumed internally: beer, cider, meat, salt, starch, hats.

At the Restoration, in 1660, direct taxation took a new form – ASSESSMENTS. Parliament fixed a particular area's tax liability and local worthies were appointed to apportion and collect it. There was also a POLL TAX that year, and again in the 1690s. This particular tax was always unpopular with the poor and had been the cause of the Peasants' Revolt in 1381. It was abandoned in 1698 and not revived again until Mrs Thatcher's ill-fated attempt in 1990. Between 1662 and 1689 there was a HEARTH TAX or CHIMNEY TAX of two shillings a hearth. In 1696 the WINDOW TAX came in – the more windows in your house, the more you paid, though cottages were exempt. It was only abolished in 1851.

In the 1690s Assessments were replaced by AIDS, under which all were taxed at the same rate regardless of area. Although nominally on personal property as well as land, Aids soon came to be known as the LAND TAX, since personal property was so easy to conceal. This was the main direct tax for more than a century. Special taxes were raised on a number of items at the end of the 17th century: stamped paper, hackney carriages, hawkers, births, deaths, marriages, bachelors, salt, tobacco pipes, stamp duty on documents. This last was the only one to become permanent.

TAXES – SINEWS OF WAR During William III's Nine Years' War with France, ending in 1697, the annual tax yield went up from £2 million to £4.8 million. During the War of the Spanish Succession in the 1700s it was consistently over £5 million. Prime Minister Robert Walpole stabilised it at £6 million during the two peaceful decades after 1720, but by the end of the Seven Years' War in 1763 it was up to £10 million, by the end of the American War of Independence £12.7 million, and by the end of the Napoleonic Wars, £68 million.

THE NATIONAL DEBT Taxes, whether direct or indirect, were not enough to pay for wars. Governments had to borrow money as well, and so the National Debt grew with each new conflict. The annual interest payable on it, ' a tax on future generations', went from £1.5 million in 1688, to £3 million in 1714, £4.7 million in 1763, £8 million in 1783, £13.6 million in 1797 and £32 million in 1815. The Debt itself, which had been £16.7 million in 1697, was £700 million by 1815.

GIN, TEA AND SMUGGLING After 1700 England was swept by an addiction to the new spirit, gin, introduced from Holland. In an attempt to control its consumption two acts were passed in 1729 and 1736 allowing it to be taxed, not as a financial but as a social measure. Tea-drinking was another new passion and it attracted the attention of the Customs men and the smugglers equally. In 1743 it was estimated that duty at four shillings a lb was collected on 650,000 lbs of tea, but that Britain's actual consumption was 1,500,000 lbs. In 1767 new duties on various items including tea were imposed on the American colonies. These were removed in 1770, except for that on tea, which gave a boost to sales of smuggled tea there. Then in 1772 the East India Company was given permission to export tea direct to America, which brought the price down sharply, severely shrinking the smugglers' market. They raised an outcry against the duty element in the price of unsmuggled tea, as an internal tax imposed by Britain without the colonists' consent, and in 1773 at the Boston Tea Party, many chests of it were thrown into the harbour. The American War of Independence followed in 1775.

INCOME TAX The National Debt went from £127 million to £231 million as a result of the American War, in spite of new taxes such as ones on male servants, legacies, fire insurance, and property sold at auction. The costs of the Napoleonic Wars forced William Pitt the Younger to introduce income tax in 1799. Incomes below £60 were exempt, there was a sliding scale to £200 and ten per cent was levied thereafter. It was abolished in 1816, but Sir Robert Peel reintroduced it in 1842 when he began his campaign to remove a whole mass of duties on goods, culminating in his Repeal of the Corn Laws in 1846. Duty on soap went in 1853 along with those on 100 other items.

CUSTOMS DUTIES remained important during this period. In 1822–24 the following items were seized from smugglers by the PREVENTIVE SERVICE, as the Customs Men were called: ' 129 vessels, 746 boats, 312 livestock, 135,000 gallons brandy, 227,000 gallons gin, 105,000 gallons whisky, 253 gallons rum, 596 gallons wine, 3,000 lbs snuff, 19,000 lbs tea, 42,000 yards silk, 21,000 Indian handkerchiefs, 36,000 packs of playing cards, 75 spirit stills, 23 Leghorn (Italian straw) hats.'

The number of carriage owners paying for a licence to be allowed to display their coats of arms on the sides of their carriages grew from under 14,000 in 1812 to over 20,000 in 1830, to a peak of 24,000 in 1841. In 1830 7,000 paid for the privilege of displaying their coats of arms on their writing paper, silver and cutlery; by 1868 the figure was 43,000.

THE SOURCES OF PUBLIC INCOME IN 1835

CUSTOMS AND EXCISE		£	£
Spirits	Foreign	1,529,540	—
	Rum	1,537,694	—
	British	5,059,197	—
Malt		4,925,521	—
Hops		324,792	—
Wine		1,691,511	—
Sugar and Molasses		4,947,670	—
Tea		3,832,432	—
Coffee		652,124	—
Tobacco and Snuff		3,334,234	—
			27,834,715
Butter		143,160	—
Cheese		70,520	—
Currants and Raisins		335,057	—
Corn		234,576	—
Cotton Wool and Sheep's imported		540,118	—
Silk		214,898	—
Hides and Skins		64,796	—
Paper		831,057	—
Soap		773,888	—
Candles and Tallow		158,876	—
Coals, sea-borne		5,061	—
Glass		663,237	—
Bricks, Tiles and Slates		399,773	—
Timber		1,394,940	—
Auctions		242,023	—
Excise Licenses		1,116,923	—
Miscellaneous Duties of Customs and Excise		1,516,998	—
			8,705,901
Total Customs and Excise			36,540,616

STAMPS		£	£
Deeds and other Instruments		1,554,999	—
Probate and Legacies		2,060,008	—
Insurance	Marine	217,058	—
	Fire	804,756	—
Bills of Exchange, Bankers' Note		663,279	—
Newspapers and Advertisements		552,039	—

Stage Coaches	498,497	—
Post Horses	241,165	—
Receipts	170,599	—
Other Stamp Duties	462,507	—
		7,224,907

ASSESSED AND LAND TAXES

		£	£
Land Taxes		1,199,783	—
Houses		57.000	—
Windows		1,204,490	—
Servants	Male servants Under gamekeepers Travellers or Riders Clerks and book-keepers Stewards, bailiffs Shopmen, warehousemen Waiters in taverns Male servants not being servants to their employers	198,454	—
Horses	Horses used for riding or drawing carriages Horses charged at modified rates Other horses and mules	386,459	—
Carriages	4-wheel carriages Post-chaises and carriages 2-wheel carriages	424,129	—
Dogs	Exclusive of packs of hounds	160,349	—
Other Assessed Taxes	Horse dealers, London Horse dealers, other places Hair powder Armorial bearings Game certificates Certificates for the sale of game	250,733	—
			3,881,397

Post Office	2,243,294
Crown Lands	382,973
Other Ordinary Revenues and other Resources	221,545

TOTAL INCOME	£ 50,494,732

THE MODERN ERA

1894 Graduated Estate (Death) Duties introduced, with a higher percentage payable the bigger the estate. This established the principle that direct tax should be heaviest for the wealthy.

1909 Lloyd George's Budget. Money was needed to pay for Old Age Pensions, just introduced, and for the Dreadnought battleships being added to the Royal Navy. Death Duties were increased, as were those on alcohol and tobacco. Income Tax went up and Super (Sur-) Tax was introduced. Cars and petrol were taxed for the first time. The unearned increment in land values was taxed, the amount being payable when the land changed hands.

1911 National Insurance introduced, workers, employers and the state all contributing. Lloyd George said that for the workers it meant 'ninepence for fourpence'.

1940 Purchase Tax introduced.

1944 PAYE introduced

1965 Capital Gains Tax and Corporation Tax introduced.

1973 Value Added Tax replaces Purchase Tax

1975 Petroleum Revenue Tax introduced as North Sea Oil began to flow.

'What with the duties expected of one during one's lifetime, and the duties exacted from one after one's death, land has ceased to be either a profit or a pleasure. It gives one position, and prevents one from keeping it up. That's all that can be said about land.'

Lady Bracknell in Oscar Wilde's The Importance of Being Earnest, *1895.*

Mr John Bull after an attack of Income tax
Punch 1848

THE INDUSTRIAL REVOLUTION

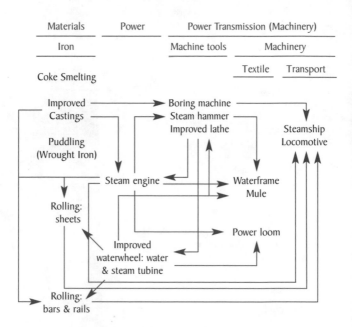

Materials	Power	Power Transmission (Machinery)		
Iron		Machine tools	Machinery	
			Textile	Transport

Coke Smelting

The diagram above, while stimulating and ingenious, is not – and not intended to be – a complete explanation of the Industrial Revolution. To get closer to that, it needs to be seen against the background formed by the particularly conducive circumstances prevalent in 18th-century Britain:

• Internal security and overseas possessions
• Improving agriculture
• Spread of the scientific method, based on observation, experiment, accuracy and measurement, together with (sometimes) close relations of scientists with industry
• Decay of restrictive monopolies, privileges and guilds, but legal protection of property
• Large internal market and absence of internal tariffs
• Advanced system of banking and credit, with falling rates of interest
• Improving communications and transport
• Plenty of coal

FINES IMPOSED ON COTTON SPINNERS

These penalties were in force in the 1800s at a mill at Tyldesley near Manchester, where spinners worked in temperatures of eighty degrees Fahrenheit or more. The amounts are in shillings.

Any spinner found with his window open	1. 0
Any spinner found dirty at his work	1. 0
Any spinner found washing himself	1. 0
Any spinner leaving his oil can out of its place	1. 0
Any spinner slipping with his gas lighted	2. 0
Any spinner putting his gas out too soon	1. 0
Any spinner spinning with gaslight too long in the morning	2. 0
Any spinner heard whistling	1. 0
Any spinner being five minutes after last bell rings	1. 0
Any spinner going further than the roving-room door when fetching rovings	1. 0
Any spinner being sick and cannot find another spinner to give satisfaction must pay for steam per day	6. 0

COTTON AND WOOL

THE COTTON INDUSTRY was divided into yarn-spinning and fabric-weaving. Spinning was located mainly in southern Lancashire, within an eleven-mile radius of Manchester.

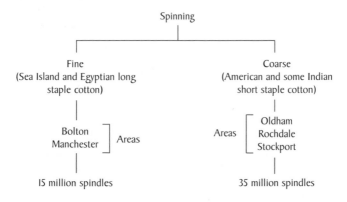

The spun yarn was then marketed at the Manchester Royal Exchange before passing to the weaving mills, mostly further north in Lancashire.

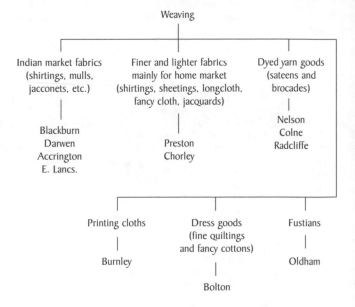

Weaving

Indian market fabrics (shirtings, mulls, jacconets, etc.)	Finer and lighter fabrics mainly for home market (shirtings, sheetings, longcloth, fancy cloth, jacquards)	Dyed yarn goods (sateens and brocades)
Blackburn Darwen Accrington E. Lancs.	Preston Chorley	Nelson Colne Radcliffe

Printing cloths	Dress goods (fine quiltings and fancy cottons)	Fustians
Burnley	Bolton	Oldham

Once woven, the fabric was bleached and printed, mainly in Lancashire and Cheshire. Dyeing was done in Yorkshire. Eighty per cent of the cotton fabrics were exported, and in 1913 they represented 24 per cent of all Britain's exports. British India and the Far East absorbed over half of this exported cotton fabric. Exports never recovered after the First World War and the industry went into a rapid decline.

THE WOOLLEN INDUSTRY was based in the West Riding of Yorkshire, which had 50 per cent of Britain's spindles and 60 per cent of her looms. (The only woollen manufacture in Lancashire was of flannel in Rochdale.) The industry was divided, not by process as was the case with cotton, but by product: Worsteds, Woollens and Shoddy. The processes of the industry are sorting, washing and scouring, combing or carding, drawing and spinning, warp dressing and weaving, dyeing and finishing. The majority of firms did two or three of these processes, but many did only one. About 40 or 50 per cent of British woollen cloth was exported in 1913 and a great deal of what was not was supplied to the ready-made clothing industry in Leeds.

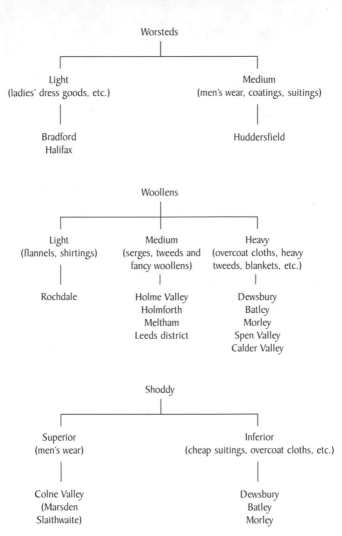

Worsteds
- Light (ladies' dress goods, etc.)
  - Bradford
  - Halifax
- Medium (men's wear, coatings, suitings)
  - Huddersfield

Woollens
- Light (flannels, shirtings)
  - Rochdale
- Medium (serges, tweeds and fancy woollens)
  - Holme Valley
  - Holmforth
  - Meltham
  - Leeds district
- Heavy (overcoat cloths, heavy tweeds, blankets, etc.)
  - Dewsbury
  - Batley
  - Morley
  - Spen Valley
  - Calder Valley

Shoddy
- Superior (men's wear)
  - Colne Valley (Marsden Slaithwaite)
- Inferior (cheap suitings, overcoat cloths, etc.)
  - Dewsbury
  - Batley
  - Morley

Hosiery, cotton and woollen goods knitted by machin were produced in Leicester and Nottingham, and machine-made lace was also a Nottingham speciality.

THE COST OF SUBSISTENCE LIVING
IN LEEDS IN 1832

'The least possible sum per week for which a man, his wife and three children can obtain a sufficiency of food, clothing and other necessaries' – *Compiled by Humphrey Boyle of Leeds, February 1832.*

Rent 2/-, fuel 9d, candle 3d	3s 0d	Brought up	14s 6½d
Soap 3d, soda 1d, blue & starch 1½d	5½d	Vegetables 1d per day	7d
Sand, black lead, bees wax etc.	2d	Salt, pepper, mustard, vinegar	2d
Whitewashing a cottage twice a year	½d	7 pts beer 1½d	10½d
1½ st flour for bread–2/6d st ¼ st flour for puddings– 2/8d st	3s 9d 8d	Water	1d
Eggs 2d, yeast 1½d	3½d	Schooling for 2 children	6d
1½ pints milk per day at 1¼d	11d	Reading	2d
¼ stone oatmeal 2/2d st	6½d	Wear & tear in beds, bedding, brushes, pots, pans & other household furniture	6d
1 lb treacle 3½d lb, 1½ lb sugar at 7d lb	1s 2d	Clothing: husband ½d, wife 8d	1s 10d
1½ oz tea at 5d, 2 oz coffee 1½d	10½d	each child 4d	1s 0d
5 lb meat 6d	2s 6d		
	14s 6½d		£1 0s 3d

'Besides the sum required for the fund which it is agreed every workman [ought] to lay in store for sickness and old age, I have set nothing down for butter, not being certain whether it is essential to health, although it is to be found in almost every cottage where the weekly income is not more than half the amount I have stated as necessary for the proper support of a family; tobacco, although it is in very general use, I have omitted for the same reason; neither have I reckoned anything for religious instruction which is thought by great numbers of the people as necessary to their happiness as is their daily bread: something, therefore, ought to be allowed for it.'

FORLORN FEMALES, PENITENT PROSTITUTES AND FLOATING CHAPELS

As the 18th century progressed, an increasing number of charitable groups emerged, particularly from the reviving evangelical wing of the Church of England. The most famous were the abolitionists, those behind the cause of anti-slavery, but the philanthropic urge in fact spread into all imaginable corners. Here are a few of the more striking from the hundreds of bodies established from the 1750s to the 1840s.

✠ The Humane Society for the Recovery of Drowned and Suffocated Persons (this evolved into the Royal Humane Society aimed at 'persons in a state of suspended animation')

✠ The National Truss Society for the Relief of the Ruptured Poor

✠ The Royal Infirmary for Sun Bathing

✠ The Magdalen Hospital for the Reception of Penitent Prostitutes

✠ The Society of Universal Good Will

✠ The Society for the Relief of Poor, Pious Clergymen, of the Established Church, Residing in the Country

✠ The Society for Carrying into Effect his Majesty's Proclamation Against Vice and Immorality

✠ The Asylum or House of Refuge, for the Reception of Orphan Girls the Settlements of Whose Parents Cannot be Found

✠ The Institution for the Protection of Young Country Girls

✠ The Society for Superseding the Necessity of Climbing Boys (chimney sweepers' apprentices)

✠ The London Society for Promoting Christianity Amongst the Jews

✠ The Society for the Diffusion of Knowledge upon the Punishment of Death, and the Improvement of Prison Discipline

✠ The Forlorn Female's Fund of Mercy

✠ The London Society for the Encouragement of Faithful Female Servants

✠ The London Orphan Asylum, for the Reception and Education of Destitute Orphans, Particularly those Descended from Respectable Parents

✠ The Downs Society of Fishermen's Friends

✠ The Provisional Protection Society of Females

✠ The Scripture Admonition Society

✠ The Association for the Refutation of Infidel Publications

✠ The British and Irish Ladies' Society for Improving the Condition and Promoting the Industry and Welfare of the Female Peasantry in Ireland

✠ The Institution for the Cure of Various Diseases by Bandages and Compression

✠ The Episcopal Floating Chapel

✠ The Society for the Investigation of Prophecy

✠ The Association for Promoting Rational Humanity Towards the Animal Creation

✠ The Society for Returning Young Women to their Friends in the Country

'I have long been addicted to the gaming table. I have lately taken to the turf. I fear I frequently blaspheme. But I have never distributed religious tracts. All this was known to you and your Society. Notwithstanding which you think me a fit person to be your president. God forgive your hypocrisy.' – *Letter written early in the 19th century by the Earl of Orford to the Norwich Bible Society.*

Interior of a West End brothel

POPULATION

The first ten-yearly public census was taken in 1801 and it showed:

England	8,479,000
Wales	541,000
Scotland	1,610,000
Ireland	5,216,000
TOTAL	15,846,000

The distribution of the English population in 1801 by counties by order of size was:

Yorkshire	858,892	Lincolnshire	208,557	Cumberland	117,230
Middlesex	818,129	Warwick	208,190	Dorset	115,319
Lancashire	672,731	Shropshire	197,639	Oxford	109,620
Devon	343,001	Cheshire	191,751	Berkshire	109,215
Kent	307,624	Cornwall	188,269	Buckingham	107,444
Somerset	273,750	Wiltshire	185,107	Hertford	97,577
Norfolk	273,371	Derbyshire	161,142	Cambridge	89,346
Surrey	269,049	Durham	160,861	Hereford	89,191
Gloucester	250,803	Sussex	159,311	Bedfordshire	63,393
Staffordshire	239,153	Northumberland	157,101	Monmouth	45,582
Essex	226,437	Nottingham	140,350	Westmorland	41,617
Hampshire	219,656	Worcester	139,333	Huntingdon	37,568
Suffolk	210,431	Northampton	131,757	Rutland	16,356
		Leicester	130,081		

THE 1811 census gave a total of 18,044,000. By 1851 the total was 27,408,000 and this in spite of the effect of the Irish potato famine of 1845–47, which resulted in the Irish population figure falling from 8,295,000 to 6,466,000, as a result of both death and emigration.

The 1851 CENSUS allowed a breakdown to be made of the population by occupation:

OCCUPATIONS	PERSONS
Agricultural labourer	1,460,896
Farm servant, shepherd	1,038,791
Cotton calico, manufacturer, printing and dyeing	561,465

Labourer (branch undefined)	376,551
Farmer, grazier	306,767
Boot and shoe maker	274,451
Milliner, dressmaker	267,791
Coal-miner	219,015
Carpenter, joiner	182,636
Army and Navy	178,773 *
Tailor	152,672
Washerwoman, mangler, laundry-keeper	146,091
Woollen cloth manufacture	137,814
Silk manufacture	114,570
Blacksmith	112,776
Worsted manufacture	104,061
Mason, pavior	101,442
Messenger, porter and errand boy	101,425
Linen, flax manufacture	98,860
Seaman (Merchant Service) on shore or in British ports	89,206
Grocer	85,913
Gardener	80,916
Iron manufacture, moulder, founder	80,032
Innkeeper, licensed victualler, beershop keeper	75,721
Seamstress, shirtmaker	73,068
Bricklayer	67,989
Butcher, meat salesman	67,691
Hose (stocking) manufacture	65,499
School, – master, mistress	65,376
Lace manufacture	63,660
Plumber, painter, glazier	62,808
Baker	62,472
Carman, carrier, carter, drayman	56,981
Charwoman	55,423
Draper (linen and woollen)	49,184
Engine and machine maker	48,082
Commercial clerk	43,760
Cabinet maker, upholsterer	40,897
Teacher (various), governess	40,575
Fisherman, woman	38,294
Boat, barge, man, woman	37,683
Miller	37,268
Earthenware manufacture	36,512
Sawyer	35,443

* This is the Army and Navy of the United Kingdom, exclusive of the Indian Army and Navy.

Railway labourer	34,306
Straw-plait manufacture	32,062
Brick maker, dealer	31,168
Government Civil Service	30,963
Hawker, pedlar	30,553
Wheelwright	30,244
Glover	29,882
Shopkeeper (branch undefined)	29,800
Horsekeeper, groom (not domestic), jockey	29,408
Nail manufacture	28,533
Iron-miner	28,088
Printer	26,024
Nurse (not domestic servant)	25,518
Shipwright, shipbuilder	25,201
Stone quarrier	23,489
Lodging-house keeper	23,089
Lead-miner	22,530
Copper-miner	22,386
Straw hat and bonnet maker	21,902
Cooper	20,215
Watch and clock maker	19,159
Brewer	18,620
Dock labourer, dock and harbour service	18,462
Clergyman of Established Church	18,587
Protestant Dissenting Minister	9,644
Police	18,348
Plasterer	17,980
Warehouse man, woman	17,861
Saddler, harness maker	17,583
Hatter, hat manufacture	16,975
Coachman (not domestic servant), guard, postboy	16,836
Law clerk	16,626
Coachmaker	16,590
Cowkeeper, milkseller	15,526
Ropemaker	15,966
Druggist	15,643
Surgeon, apothecary	15,163
Tin-miner	15,050
Paper manufacture	14,501
Coalheaver, coal labourer	14,426
Greengrocer, fruiterer	14,320
Muslin manufacture	14,098
Confectioner	13,865
Tinman, tinker, tin-plate worker	13,770

Staymaker	13,690
Solicitor, attorney, Writer to the Signet	13,256
Dyer, scourer, calenderer	12,964
Currier	12,920
Builder	12,818
Farm bailiff	12,805
Hair-dresser, wig-maker	12,173
Coal merchant, dealer	12,092
Glass manufacture	12,005
Carpet and rug manufacture	11,457
Goldsmith, silversmith	11,242
Brass founder, moulder, manufacture	11,230
Maltster	11,150
Railway officer, clerk, station master	10,948
Bookbinder	10,953
Road labourer	10,923
Wine and spirit merchant	10,467
Fishmonger	10,439
Merchant	10,256
Ribbon manufacture	10,074

Not included in this list are any figures for those in domestic service. In 1851 these amounted to 13.3 per cent of the occupied population. The minimum number of servants that it was necessary to employ in order to claim that yours was the household of a gentleman was three. With increasing middle class prosperity in the second half of the century the numbers employed in domestic service rose to a peak of nearly 16 per cent of the occupied population in 1891.

FEMALE DOMESTICS, 1851

General servants	575,000
Housekeepers	46,500
Cooks	44,000
Housemaids	50,000
Nurserymaids	35,000
Total	750,500

MALE

Indoor General	74,000
Grooms	15,000
Coachmen	7,000
Total	96,000

A farm labourer

PARLIAMENTARY ELECTIONS

In the unreformed House of Commons before 1832 there were 82 English COUNTY members, elected by the FORTY SHILLING FREEHOLDERS – those whose annual revenue from their land came to more than that amount. There were two seats for each county and most elections were uncontested because the prominent county families agreed in advance how things should be arranged, one seat going to a Tory and one to a Whig, for example. These families were very anxious to avoid a contest because it could prove ruinously expensive. The contested Yorkshire election of 1807 cost the three candidates half a million pounds. Many of the 403 English Borough members also had to dip deep into their pockets to secure their seats. This 'Bill of Costs for a late Tory Election in the West' appeared in the *Flying Post* newspaper in January 1715. It is a caricature, but not a gross one.

£ 20	For bespeaking and collecting a mob
£ 30	Item for many suits of knots [ribbons] for their heads
£ 40	For scores of huzza-men
£ 40	For roarers of 'the Church'
£ 40	For a set of 'No Roundhead' roarers
£ 30	For several gallons of Tory punch on Church tombstones
£ 20	For a majority of clubs and brandy bottles
£ 10	For bellringers, fiddlers, and porters
£ 40	For a set of coffee-house praters
£ 50	For extraordinary expense for cloths and laced hats on show days to dazzle the mob
£ 40	For Dissenters' damners
£ 200	For demolishing two houses
£ 200	For committing two riots
£ 40	For secret encouragement to the rioters
£ 100	For a dozen perjury men
£ 50	For packing and carriage paid to Gloucester
£ 20	For breaking windows
£ 40	For a gang of aldermen abusers
£ 50	For a set of notorious liars
£ 100	For pot ale
£ 300	For law and charges in the King's Bench
£ 1.460	TOTAL

In 1784 the playwright RICHARD BRINSLEY SHERIDAN, an ardent Whig crony of the opposition leader Charles James Fox, was re-elected as an MP for Stafford. His expenses then, and in the six years that Parliament subsequently sat, were calculated for him.

	£	s	d	£	s	d
Expenses at the Borough of Stafford for election, anno 1784, 248 burgesses paid £5 5s 0d each				1,302	0	0
Yearly expenses since:– House rent and taxes	23	6	6			
Servant at 6s per week, boardwages	15	12	0			
Ditto, yearly wages	8	0	0			
Coals, etc.	11	0	0			
	57	18	6			
Ale tickets	40	0	0			
Half the members' plate	25	0	0			
Swearing young burgesses	10	0	0			
Subscription to the Infirmary	5	5	0			
Ditto clergymen's widows	2	2	0			
Ringers	4	4	0			
	86	11	0			
One year	144	9	6			
Multiplied by 6 years				866	17	0
Total expense of six years' parliament, exclusive of expenses incurred during the time of election, and your own annual expenses				2,168	17	0

Borough members were elected by different types of elector to the Forty Shilling Freeholders who elected the County members: SCOT-AND-LOT electors qualified by paying poor rates, POTWALLOPERS by being self-supporting and not in receipt of poor relief (able to keep their own cooking pot on the boil). In BURGAGE boroughs electors had to either own a burgage tenure or be a tenant under one, this being an old-fashioned form of landholding dating back to feudal times. In CORPORATION boroughs electors had to have become members of the corporation, co-opted onto it by those already members. In FREEMAN boroughs they had to be members of the guilds or 'companies' in the town, but did not have to reside there.

These different franchises were particularly open to manipulation when the numbers eligible to vote were small. A survey in 1817 claimed that of the Borough seats, 14 were in the patronage of the government; 197 borough MPs were in the House of Commons thanks to nomination by an aristocratic patron; and in another 119 boroughs the influence of a patron had been decisive in the election result. Ten years later another observer put the total somewhat lower, at 276 seats. Defenders of the system argued that its very corruption enabled members of newly emergent classes to obtain seats. In the 1818 Parliament there were over 50 bankers, merchants and businessmen. It was also true that brilliant young men were put into seats by aristocratic patrons much earlier than might otherwise have been the case. At the same time, Manchester, Birmingham and Leeds, with a combined population of nearly half a million in the 1820s, had not a single MP between them.

Bossiney, Dunwich, Hastings, New Romney, Orford, Rye, St Germans, St Mawes and Winchilsea all had fewer than 20 electors. There were nine electors in Camelford in Cornwall and the Duke of Bedford owned all the houses there, enabling him to sell the borough and its seat in 1812 for £32,000. At Gatton in Surrey there was only one elector and it was sold several times, lastly in 1830, for a reputed £180,000. Old Sarum was particularly notorious. The Earl of Caledon owned the seven uninhabited burgage tenures there and so could nominate its two MPs. In Stockbridge the 57 electors refused to pay rent or give their vote until they each were paid £60. At Malmesbury, population 1,000, of the 13 members of its Corporation who formed the electorate, ten were incapable of signing an official document. However, the local chemist acted as their agent, offering the town's two seats at a fixed price. At Marlborough the corporation was said to have consisted of the Marquess of Ailesbury's steward, butler, footmen and dependants. At Carlisle Lord Lonsdale was master of the corporation and got it to make freemen 14,000 of the men working in his mines. With the votes of these he was able to wrest the seat away from the Duke of Norfolk. Sir Robert Peel's father bought control of Tamworth from two local families. The final irony is that Lords Radnor and Fitzwilliam, both borough proprietors, formed, with their clientele in the House of Commons, the backbone of the majority in favour of reform in 1832.

'I received yours and am surprised at your insolence in troubling me about the Excise. You know, what I very well know, that I bought you. And I know what perhaps you think I don't know, you are now selling yourselves to Someone Else; and I know what you do not know, that I am buying another borough. May God's curse light upon you all; may your houses be as open and common to all Excise Officers as your wives and daughters were to me, when I stood for your scoundrell corporation.' – *Letter from Anthony Henley, Member of Parliament for Southampton from 1727 to 1734, to his constituents after they had complained about the Excise Bill, which he supported.*

NELSON'S NAVY

——— CLASSIFICATION OF THE NAVY, 1793–1815 ———

SHIPS		GUNS	MEN
POSTCAPTAINS			
First Rates		100+ guns on 3 gundecks	841
Second Rates	*Line-of-battle*	90 to 98 guns on 3 gundecks	743
Third Rates		80,74 or 64 guns on 2 gundecks	493–724
Fourth Rates	*Below the line*	50 guns on 1 or 2 gundecks	345
Fifth Rates		32 to 44 guns on 1 gundeck	217–297
Sixth Rates	*Frigates*	20 to 28 guns on 1 gundeck	138–198
COMMANDERS			
Ship-sloops – *Unrated*		to 22 guns on 1 gundeck	121–135
VESSELS			
Brig-sloops – *Unrated*		to 28 guns on 1 gundeck	80–121
LIEUTENANTS			
Others – *Unrated*		to 18 guns on 1 gundeck	Varied

In 1803 Britain possessed 104 ships of the line in commission, 98 ships of the line in ordinary, or being constructed, making a total of 202 ships. France had only 39 which, combined with the Dutch and Spanish fleets, made a total of 118.

——— NELSON'S FLEET AT TRAFALGAR, 1805 ———

GUNS	SHIP	
100	Victory	Vice-admiral (White) Lord Nelson, KB
		Captain Thomas Masterman Hardy
	Royal-Sovereign	Vice-admiral (Blue) Cuthbert Collingwood
		Captain Edward Rotheram
	Britannia	Rear-admiral (White) the Earl of Northesk
		Captain Charles Bullen
98	Téméraire	Captain Eliab Harvey
	Prince	Captain Richard Grindall
	Neptune	Captain Thomas Francis Fremantle
	Dreadnought	Captain John Conn
80	Tonnant	Captain Charles Tyler

GUNS	SHIP	
	Belleisle	Captain William Hargood
	Revenge	Captain Robert Moorsom
	Mars	Captain George Duff
	Spartiate	Captain Sir Francis Laforey, Bart.
	Defiance	Captain Philip Charles Durham
	Conqueror	Captain Israel Pellow
	Defence	Captain George Hope
74	Colossus	Captain James Nicoll Morris
	Leviathan	Captain Henry William Bayntun
	Achille	Captain Richard King
	Bellerophon	Captain John Cooke
	Minotaur	Captain Charles John Moore Mansfield
	Orion	Captain Edward Codrington
	Swiftsure	Captain William George Rutherford
	Ajax	Lieutenant John Pilfold (acting)
	Thunderer	Lieutenant John Stockham (acting)
	Polyphemus	Captain Robert Redmill
64	Africa	Captain Henry Digby
	Agamemnon	Captain Sir Edward Berry

FRIGATES, Euryalus, Naiad, Phoebe, and Sirius; Captains the Hon. Henry Blackwood, Thomas Dundas, the Hon. Thomas Bladen Capel, and William Prowse. SCHOONER, Pickle, Lieutenant John Richards Lapenotiere, and CUTTER Entreprenante, Lieutenant John Puver.

Only 8 of his 27 captains at Trafalgar had ever served under Nelson before and most had never met him before he took up his command three weeks earlier. Only five had previously fought in a line-of-battle fleet action. The average age of the British crews was just under 22, and that is taking senior officers into account. There were 68 young boys on the Victory alone, and two sailors on the Neptune each took their sons, aged 9 and 10, to Trafalgar.

——— THE FRANCO-SPANISH FLEET AT TRAFALGAR ———

33 ships of the line, including the Santissima-Trinidad, 130, Principe-de-Asturias, 112, Santa-Ana, 112, Rayo, 100 and Bucentaure, Formidable, Neptune, Indomptable, Neptuno, Argonauta, 80.

After Trafalgar the Royal Navy increased in size to 250 ships while the combined Franco-Spanish-Dutch fleet shrank to 92 ships. However, between 1793 and 1815, 83 British ships of the line and 162 frigates were in fact vessels originally captured from the French or their allies. The British fleet was bedevilled by a lack

of standardisation and its home-built ships had short lives, reckoned at fifteen years at most, and sometimes at eight or less. Such defects were however compensated for by the assurance and fighting spirit of the officers and crews and the confidence placed in them by the people.

In 1794 Lord Minto, then governor of Corsica, said the naval officers there were full of life and action while with the army officers, 'It is all high lounge and still life.'

In 1801 the names of the gunboats under Nelson's command in the Channel are redolent of the aggressive ethos suffusing the Navy: Cracker, Boxer, Flamer, Haughty, Attack, Plumper, Bruiser, Wolfe, Griper, Conflict, Archer, Vixen, Minx, Bold, Locust, Jackall, Constant, Monkey, Mariner, Mallard, Snipe, Charger, Ferriter. These boats would typically have mounted two 24-pounders in the bows and ten 18-pounder carronades, and had 50-man crews.

In 1803 Admiral Earl St Vincent said, 'I do not say the French cannot come. I only say they cannot come by sea.'

In 1806 Captain Lord Cochrane advertised for extra crew for his ship the Imperieuse: 'WANTED – Stout, able-bodied men who can run a mile without stopping with a sackful of Spanish dollars on their backs.'

In 1813 the artist Benjamin Robert Haydon recalled, 'From infancy seeing French frigates sailing into Plymouth harbour, dismasted, and running along the seashore, cheering till my throat was parched.'

In 1905 Admiral Togo destroyed the Russian Baltic fleet at the Battle of Tsushima off Japan on 27 May after it had sailed halfway round the world, so winning the Russo-Japanese War. As a young man Togo had trained in Britain for seven years and his admiration for Nelson's Navy was so profound that he delayed the return of the Japanese fleet to its home port until the hundredth anniversary of Trafalgar, October 21.

In 1914 came perhaps the strangest testimony: the table at which Kaiser Wilhelm II of Germany sat in August that year to sign the mobilization of the Imperial army and navy was made of oak from Nelson's *Victory* and on it was a stand for stationery in the form of a model of the ship, flying the flags spelling out the famous signal, 'England expects . . .'

DEATHS IN THE PENINSULAR WAR
AND AT WATERLOO

This table of total deaths among officers and men in the Peninsular army from the beginning of 1811 until 25th May 1814, demonstrates that nearly three times as many other ranks died of disease and privation as died in or as a result of battle. The British army in Spain of 61,511 men had 13,815, or 22.5 per cent, constantly sick during this period, while sickness from wounds did not amount to more than 1.5 per cent. There were fewer field officers and captains than lieutenants, but they suffered proportionately much higher casualty rates.

RANK	Total deaths during 41 months	Probable distribution of these deaths		Mortality from all causes per cent per annum
		Killed and died of wounds	Death from disease and privation	
Field Officers	87	56	31	16.2
Captains	239	168	71	12.9
Subalterns	517	315	202	9.5
Staff	97	27	70	6.8
Total Officers	940	566	374	10.1
Total Privates	33,829	8,899	24,930	16.1

The Waterloo campaign was over too soon for disease, the weather and short supplies of bad food to really do their work. But the battle itself was 'a damned serious business', in the words of the Duke of Wellington. He had between 24,000 and 26,000 British troops, 5,800 soldiers of the King's German Legion (in fact recruited from every European country except France, Italy and Spain, though most of its officers were German), and 37,000 Hanoverians, Brunswickers, Dutch and Belgians. Overall casualties were between 15,000 and 16,000, of which 6,729 were British. In percentage terms this was worse than the Somme in 1916. Of the 840 British officers present 85 were killed and 365 wounded. (Ten were 'missing', of whom most were later found to be dead.) The 27th Foot (Iniskillings) suffered worst: out of 740, only 157 men and one officer were unwounded by the end.

BRITISH LOANS AND SUBSIDIES TO FOREIGN STATES DURING THE WARS OF 1793–1814

The contributions made to the defeat of Napoleon by the Royal Navy and by the Army under Wellington in the Iberian Peninsula tend to overshadow the part played by Britain's financing of the forces of her Continental allies. This policy, begun by Pitt the Elder in the Seven Years' War in the middle of the 18th century, was continued by Pitt the Younger and his successors from 1793 onwards. Someone disobligingly characterised it at the time as 'breaking windows with guineas'.

1793		
Hanover	492,650	——
Hesse-Cassel	190,623	——
Sardinia	150,000	——
....		833,273

1794		
Prussia	1,226,495	——
Sardinia	200,000	——
Hesse-Cassel	437,105	——
Hesse-		——
Darmstadt	102,073	——
Baden	25,196	——
Hanover	559,376	——
....		2,550,245

1795		
Germany,		
Imperial Loan	4,600,000	——
Baden	1,794	——
Brunswick	97,722	——
Hesse-Cassel	317,492	——
Hesse-		
Darmstadt	79,605	——
Hanover	478,348	——
Sardinia	150,000	——
....		5,724,961

1796		
		——
Hesse-		——
Darmstadt	20,076	——
Brunswick	12,794	——
....		32,870

1797		
Brunswick	7,571	——
Hesse-		
Darmstadt	57,015	——
Germany		
Imperial Loan	1,620,000	——
....		1,684,596

1798		
Brunswick	7,000	——
Portugal	120,013	——
....		127,013

1799		
Prince of		
Orange	20,000	——
Hesse-		
Darmstadt	4,812	——
Russia	825,000	——
....		849,812

1800		
Germany	1,066,666	——
German Princes	500,000	——
Bavaria	501,017	——
Russia	545,494	——
....		2,613,177

1801		
Portugal	200,114	——
Sardinia	40,000	——
Hesse-Cassel	100,000	——

Germany	150,000	—
German Princes	200,000	—
....		690,114
1802		
Hesse-Cassel	33,451	—
Sardinia	52,000	—
Russia	200,000	—
....		285,451
1803		
Hanover	117,628	—
Russia	63,000	—
Portugal	31,647	—
....		212,275
1804		
Sweden	20,119	—
Hesse-Cassel	83,304	—
....		103,423
1805		
Hanover	35,341	—
....		35,341
1806		
Hanover	76,865	—
Hesse-Cassel	18,982	—
Germany	500,000	—
....		595,847
1807		
Hanover	19,899	—
Russia	614,183	—
Hesse-Cassel	45,000	—
Prussia	180,000	—
....		859,082
1808		
Spain	1,497,873	—
Sweden	1,100,000	—
Sicily	300,000	—
....		2,897,873

1809		
Spain	529,039	—
Portugal	600,000	—
Sweden	300,000	—
Sicily	300,000	—
Austria	850,000	—
....		2,579,039
1810		
Hesse-Cassel	45,150	—
Spain	402,875	—
Portugal	1,237,518	—
Sicily	425,000	—
....		2,110,543
1811		
Spain	220,690	—
Portugal	1,832,168	—
Sicily	275,000	—
Portuguese Sufferers	39,555	—
....		2,367,413
1812		
Spain	1,000,000	—
Portugal	2,167,832	—
Portuguese Sufferers	60,445	—
Sicily	400,000	—
Sweden	278,292	—
Morocco	1,952	—
....		3,908,521
1813		
Spain	1,000,000	—
Portugal	1,644,063	—
Sicily	600,000	—
Sweden	1,320,000	—
Russia	657,500	—
Russian Sufferers	200,000	—
Prussia	650,040	—
Prince of Orange	200,000	—

Austria	500,000	——	Russia	2,169,982	——
Morocco	14,419	——	Prussia	1,319,129	——
		6,786,022	Austria	1,064,882	——
			France (advanced		
1814			to Louis XVIII to		
Spain	450,000	——	enable him to		
Portugal	1,500,000	——	return to France)	200,000	——
Sicily	316,667	——	Hanover	500,000	——
Sweden	800,000	——	Denmark	121,918	——
					8,442,578

TOTAL 46,289,459

By Germany is meant the Holy Roman Empire centred on Vienna, covering much of central Europe and stretching into the Balkans and Italy, also including much of Germany. It was finally abolished at the insistence of Napoleon in 1806.

―――――――― **NON-MONETARY TRANSACTIONS, 1814** ――――――――

Over and above these payments, arms, clothing and stores were also regularly sent by Britain to her allies. The scale of these non-monetary transactions can be grasped from the figures below, for the single year of 1814.

Austria – Arms and Clothing	410,751
France – Arms sent to the South of France	31,932
Hanover – Arms and Clothing	239,879
Holland – Arms and Clothing	267,759
Oldenburg – Clothing	10,008
Prussia – Arms	11,042
Russia – Provisions and Stores	385,491
Spain – Stores	136,338
Miscellaneous – Arms and Clothing supplied to various foreign corps	88,845

TOTAL 1,582,045

Early in 1814 Castlereagh, the British Foreign Secretary, claimed that his country's contribution to the allied war effort was the equivalent of 425,000 men: £5 million of subsidies to Prussia, Austria and Russia was the equivalent of 150,000 troops; there were 90,000 British troops in the field; and the £6.6 million going in subsidies to smaller allies made up the difference. This was almost as much as the three major powers combined.

ENGLAND'S MAJOR VICTORIES OVER FRANCE

1106 Battle of Tinchebrai	the Normans of Normandy defeated by Henry I
1198 Battle of Gisors	Richard I's parole for the day is 'Dieu et Mon Droit'
1202 Battle of Mirabeau	King John captures Arthur of Brittany
1213 Battle of Damme	English fleet defeats French invaders
1217 Battle of Lincoln	William Marshal beats Prince Louis of France
1217 Battle of Dover	French fleet destroyed by Hubert de Burgh
1293 Sack of La Rochelle	Cinque Ports fleet defeats Normans and sacks the port
1340 Battle of Sluys	Sea battle at start of the 100 Years' War
1346 Battle of Crecy	Knights and archers of England defeat the chivalry of France
1347 Surrender of Calais	Burghers spared after Edward III's queen pleads for their lives
1356 Battle of Poitiers	Another victory for English archers
1415 Battle of Agincourt	Another victory for English archers
1416 Battle of Harfleur	Duke of Bedford captures 500 French ships
1424 Battle of Verneuil	One-third of French knighthood killed by English, under the Duke of Bedford, and Burgundians
1429 Battle of the Herrings	Sir John Fastolf's archers defeat the Duc de Bourbon
1513 Battle of the Spurs	French use 'their spurs more than their swords', near Calais
1689 Battle of Walcourt	First Anglo-French battle for many years at start of Nine Years' War against Louis XIV
1692 Battle of La Hogue	Admirals Russell and Rooke are victorious
1704 Battle of Blenheim	Marlborough's first great victory in the War of the Spanish Succession
1706 Battle of Ramillies	Marlborough's second victory
1706 Surrender of Antwerp	
1708 Battle of Oudenarde	Marlborough's third victory
1708 Surrender of Lille	
1709 Surrender of Ghent	
1709 Surrender of Tournai	
1709 Battle of Malplaquet	Marlborough's fourth victory
1710 Surrender of Douai	
1710 Surrender of Bouchain	
1710 Surrender of Mons	
1743 Battle of Dettingen	The War of the Austrian Succession
1745 Surrender of Louisberg	Stronghold on Cape Breton Island in Gulf of St Lawrence, Canada

1747 First Battle of Finisterre	Anson annihilates squadron under La Jonquière
1747 Second Battle of Finisterre	Hawke orders every captain to engage at pistol shot range – fifty yards
1751 Arcot	Clive captures then holds S. Indian fortress against attacks by Indian allies of the French
1755 Battle of Lake George	Defeat of French and Indian allies in Mohawk Valley
1757 Battle of Plassey	Clive strikes blow at French influence in Bengal
1758 Capture of Louisberg	for second time
1758 Capture of Fort Duquesne	Taken by Col Forbes and renamed Pittsburg
1759 Capture of Forts Niagara	and Ticonderoga
1759 Battle of Minden	Ferdinand of Brunswick in command of combined British and Hanoverian forces
1759 Battle of Lagos	Boscawen, off the Algarve
1759 Capture of Quebec	Wolfe dies after scaling Heights of Abraham
1759 Battle of Quiberon Bay	Hawke, off Brittany
1760 Battle of Wandewash	Coote defeats Lally in Madras
1760 Surrender of Montreal	
1760 Battle of Warburg	Granby charges bareheaded
1761 Battle of Vellinghausen	
1778 Capture of Pondicherry	Loss ends French presence in India
1782 Battle of the Saints	Rodney, off Dominica
1793 Battle of Lincelles	
1794 Battle of the Glorious First of June	Howe, off Ushant
1798 Battle of the Nile	Nelson, off Egypt
1799 Siege of Acre	Sidney Smith repulses French in Syria
1800 Capture of Malta	
1801 Battle of Alexandria	French army in Egypt surrenders
1801 Battle in Algeciras Bay	Sammarez against Franco–Spanish squadron
1805 Battle of Trafalgar	
1805 Trafalgar Postscript	Strachan captures four French battleships that escaped from Trafalgar
1806 Battle of Occa Bay	Duckworth defeats Leissegues off San Domingo and destroys three battleships
1806 Battle of Maida	Gen. Stuart in Calabria
1808 Battle of Rolica	Wellington's first victory in the Peninsula, in Portugal
1808 Battle of Vimiero	Wellington in Portugal
1809 Battle of Oporto	Wellington defeats Soult, in Portugal
1809 Battle of Talavera	Wellington in Spain
1810 Battle of Busaco	Wellington in Portugal
1810 Capture of Mauritius	In Indian Ocean

1811 Battle of Barrosa	Gen. Graham in Spain
1811 Battle of Fuentes de Onoro	Wellington in Spain
1811 Battle of Albuera	Marshal Beresford in Spain
1812 Capture of Ciudad Rodrigo	Wellington, Spanish fortress
1812 Capture of Badajoz	Wellington, Spanish fortress
1812 Battle of Salamanca	Wellington defeats Marmont
1813 Battle of Vittoria	Wellington defeats Jourdan
1813 Capture of San Sebastian	Wellington, Spanish fortress
1813 Crossing of Bidassoa	River marking French border with Spain
1813 Crossing of Nivelle	In France
1814 Battle of Orthez	
1814 Battle of Toulouse	
1815 Battle of Waterloo	
1898 Fashoda Incident	Marchand gives way to Kitchener on the Upper Nile
1940 Mers-El-Kebir and Oran	French fleet shelled after ultimatum, to remove risk of it falling into German hands
1941 Surrender of Syria and Lebanon	Vichy French Middle East possessions
1942 Surrender of Madagascar	By Vichy French
1942 Surrender of Algeria and Morocco	
1942 Surrender of Dakar	

Before the Crimean War, there were very few occasions when the French and British fought as allies. It happened in 1658 when the French and men of Cromwell's New Model Army campaigned against the Spanish in the Low Countries (though there were also English Royalist exiles fighting with the Spanish) and, most memorably, in 1673 against the Dutch at the siege of Maastrict. When the Dutch mounted a surprise counter-attack the day was saved by a small group including Charles II's bastard son, the Duke of Monmouth, the young John Churchill, later the Duke of Marlborough, some twelve Life Guards and a group of French musketeers led by a certain M. d'Artagnan, the original of Dumas' hero, who lost his life that day.

THE PURCHASE OF COMMISSIONS IN THE ARMY

In 1855 there was much anger at the incompetence shown by the British generals in the Crimean War. This led to a call for an end to the system by which commissions, and thus promotion, could be purchased in the Army. The Prime Minister, Lord Palmerston, defended the practice on the grounds that it had produced some excellent officers and resulted in command of the Army resting with members of the landed aristocracy. This prevented the formation of a professional military caste which might pose a threat to civil liberty. His argument was one he had inherited from the Duke of Wellington, a staunch defender of purchase, and it was sufficient to delay the abolition of the system until 1871. The tariff below shows the prices of commissions in 1821. By adding up the sets of figures in the right-hand column, the totals needed to progress from cornet or ensign to lieutenant-colonel can be worked out. Commissions and promotion in the Royal Navy could not be bought; officers had to rely on 'a bloody war and a sickly season' (one of the toasts they drank among themselves) to create gaps in the ranks above them which they could then fill.

Commissions	Prices (£)	Difference in value between the several commissions in succession (£)
ROYAL REGIMENT OF HORSE GUARDS		
Cornet	1,200	—
Lieutenant	1,600	400
Captain	3,500	1,900
Major	5,350	1,850
Lieutenant-Colonel	7,250	1,900
LIFE-GUARDS		
Cornet	1,260	—
Lieutenant	1,785	525
Captain	3,500	1,715
Major	5,350	1,850
Lieutenant-Colonel	7,250	1,900
DRAGOON GUARDS AND DRAGOONS		
Cornet	840	—
Lieutenant	1,190	350

Captain	3,225	2,085
Major	4,575	1,350
Lieutenant-Colonel	6,175	1,600

FOOT GUARDS

Ensign	1,200	—
Lieutenant	2,050	850
Captain, with rank of Lieutenant-Colonel	4,800	2,750
Major, with rank of Colonel	8,300	3,500
Lieutenant-Colonel	9,000	700

FUSILEERS AND RIFLE REGIMENTS

| Second Lieutenant | 500 | — |
| First Lieutenant | 700 | — |

MARCHING REGIMENTS OF FOOT

Ensign	453	—
Lieutenant	700	250
Captain	1,800	1,100
Major	3,200	1,400
Lieutenant-Colonel	4,500	1,300

SENTENCE OF DEATH

In 1818, at a time when there were more than 200 capital offences, a Special Committee was set up to consider the repeal of those, either nearly so indifferent as to require no penalty, or if injurious, not of such a magnitude that they may not safely be left punishable as misdemeanours at common law.'

1 & 2 Phil. & Mary, c.4	Egyptians [gypsies] remaining within the kingdom one month.
18 Ch.II, c.3	Notorious thieves in Cumberland & Northumberland.
9 Geo.I, c.22	Being armed and disguised in any forest, park etc.
9 Geo.I, c.22	Being armed and disguised in any warren.
	Being armed and disguised in any high road, open heath, common or down.
	Unlawfully hunting, killing, or stealing deer.
	Robbing warrens, etc.
	Stealing or taking any fish out of any river or pond etc.
	Hunting in H.M.'s forests or chases.
9 Geo.I, c.28	Breaking down the head or mound of a fish pond.
12 Geo.II c.29	Being disguised within the Mint.
	Injuring Westminster Bridge & other bridges by other acts.

'The second class consists of those offences, which, though in the opinion of your Committee never fit to be punished with death, are yet so malignant and dangerous as to require the highest punishments except death which are known to our laws. These the Committee would make punishment either by transportation, or imprisonment with hard labour...'

31 Eliz. c.9	Taking away any maid, widow, or wife etc.
21 Jac. I, c.26	Acknowledging or procuring any fine, recovery, etc.
4 Geo. I, c.2	Helping to the recovery of stolen goods.
9 Geo. I, c.22	Maliciously killing or wounding cattle.
9 Geo. I, c.22	Cutting down or destroying trees growing etc.
5 Geo.II, c.30	Bankrupts not surrendering, etc.
5 Geo II, c.30	Concealing or embezzling.
6 Geo.II, c.37	Cutting down the bank of any river.
8 Geo.II, c 20	Destroying any fence, lock, sluice, etc.
26 Geo.II, c.23	Making a false entry in a marriage register, etc, five felonies
27 Geo.II, c.15	Sending threatening letters.
27 Geo.II c.19	Destroying bank, etc. Bedford Level.

3 Geo.III c.16	Personating out-pensioners of Greenwich Hospital.
22 Geo.III c.40	Maliciously cutting serges.
24 Geo.III, c.47	Harbouring offenders against that (Revenue) Act returned from transportation.

In the 1820s Robert Peel, when Home Secretary, carried five statutes exempting about 100 felonies from the death penalty. In 1832 housebreaking, horse-stealing, sheep-stealing, and coining of false money ceased to be capital offences and by 1841 there were only eight left. After 1838 no person was hanged for the rest of the century, except for murder, or, up to 1861, for attempted murder. The overall picture in relation to the death penalty and to actual executions is shown in the table below:

NUMBERS SENTENCED TO DEATH AND THOSE ACTUALLY HANGED 1814 TO 1834

CRIMES	1814–20 Sentenced	1814–20 Executed	1821–27 Sentenced	1821–27 Executed	1828–34 Sentenced	1828–34 Executed
Arson, and other wilful burning	43	19	47	9	116	59
Burglary	1,765	111	2,134	108	833	14
Breaking into a dwelling house and larceny	783	5	998	7	3,103	33
Cattle stealing	142	3	142	—	123	—
Feloniously killing and maiming	4	1	4	—	2	—
Coining	52	2	27	8	13	2
Coin, uttering counterfeit (having been convicted as common utterers)	18	—	7	—	30	—
Forgery, and uttering forged instruments	393	111	243	33	159	11
Horse stealing	651	9	902	34	628	12
Larceny, grand	1	—	4	—	—	—
in a dwelling house, etc.	892	20	1,231	26	422	5
in a shop, etc.	238	—	8	—	—	—
on a navigable river, etc.	20	4	1	—	—	—
of naval stores, etc.	20	—	—	—	—	—
Letters, containing bank notes, etc. secreting and stealing	14	4	6	2	15	1
sending threatening, etc.	2	—	4	—	—	—

CRIMES	1814–20		1821–27		1828–34	
	Sentenced	Executed	Sentenced	Executed	Sentenced	Executed
Murder	141	122	113	97	105	90
shooting at, stabbing, wounding, and administering poison, with intent to murder, etc.	93	29	146	28	327	51
Piracy	4	4	2	—	4	2
Rape, etc.	46	28	57	27	63	26
Riot and felony	—	—	50	1	159	6
Robbery of the person, on the highway, and other places	774	107	976	86	1,425	43
Sacrilege	27	2	34	—	62	—
Sheep-stealing, and killing with intent to steal	854	44	727	16	786	8
Sodomy	26	15	13	12	28	12
Transports being at large, etc.	41	—	47	—	49	—
Treason, high	56	8	1	—	1	—
Felony, transferring a stamp to defraud, etc.	—	—	—	—	1	—
cutting down trees	—	—	—	—	—	—
growing, etc.	2	1	2	—	—	—
stealing woollen cloth from a tenter	2	—	—	—	—	—
stealing part of wreck	1	—	2	—	—	—
cutting hop-binds, growing, etc.	1	—	—	—	—	—
rescuing felons	—	—	4	—	—	—
assembling armed to assist smugglers	—	—	20	—	24	—
frame breaking and destroying machinery	1	—	—	—	—	—
receiving bank notes stolen from letters	—	—	—	—	2	—
Trafficking in slaves	—	—	—	—	3	—
TOTAL NUMBER OF PERSONS IN EACH SEVEN YEARS	7,107	649	7,952	494	8,483	375

SAIL AND STEAM

1802 Charlotte Dundas paddle steamer tows boats on the Forth–Clyde canal

1804 Richard Trevithick's steam locomotive runs on the Penydarren tramway in S. Wales

1807 Clermont, the first passenger-carrying steamer, built in the USA by Robert Fulton using a Boulton and Watt engine, carries passengers along the Hudson River

1808 Wrought-iron rails start to be substituted for cast-iron ones to avoid breaks

1812 Comet, 25 tons, is the first passenger-carrying steamer in Britain, operating out of Glasgow on the Clyde

1815 Marjory, 70 tons, operates London to Gravesend service on the Thames

1816 Elise is the first steam packet to cross the Channel, from Newhaven

1816 Hibernia starts service from Holyhead in Anglesey to Ireland

1819 Savannah, an American ship with auxiliary engines, crosses from New York to Liverpool in 29 days, but only steams for 85 hours during the voyage

1821 Rising Star, a British steam warship, crosses the Atlantic from east to west, though mostly under sail, and then goes to Valparaiso in Chile to become the first steamship in the Pacific

1825 By now there are 45 steamship companies registered in London alone, but it is three times as expensive to build a steamship as a sailing vessel, coal not only costs money but takes up a great deal of space that could otherwise be filled with cargo, and the inefficiencies of the steam engines of the day mean that there need to be regular coaling depots on any long-distance route. Meanwhile, smaller crews thanks to improvements in sails and rigging, improved harbours and docks, and the disappearance of multiple ownership with the development of marine insurance have all helped to reduce freight costs on sailing ships. These factors mean that steam is uneconomic for cargo-carrying, and for the moment its future lies with passengers and mail.

1825 Stockton to Darlington Railway promoted by colliery owners in N. Yorkshire who want to get their coal to the river Tees, but also carries passengers

1825 Enterprise, 479 tons, sails and steams to Calcutta. Thereafter is successfully used on the Calcutta–Rangoon run. In 1830s steamship service run by the East India Company between Suez and Bombay commences

1829 Rocket wins steam locomotive trial at Rainhill thanks to Robert Stephenson combining three vital innovations, none of them his own invention: the multi-tubular boiler (greatly increasing the heating surface in contact with the water in the boiler), the blast pipe, and direct drive from piston to wheel

1830 Liverpool to Manchester Railway is opened

1837 Peninsular Steam Navigation Co. gets a mail contract to Spain and Portugal; in 1840 their service is extended to Malta and Alexandria and their name is changed to Peninsular and Oriental (P&O); from 1842 they run a service from Suez to Madras and Calcutta

1838 Great Western steamship, 1320 tons, is completed and begins a transatlantic service which makes the first attempt at regularity. It can reach New York in fifteen days

1838 London and Birmingham Railway opens. It has cost £53,000 a mile to build. By now there are 500 miles of railway in Britain. There will be 2,000 miles by 1844

1840 Britannia, the first steamship belonging to the Cunard Line, sails from Liverpool to Halifax and Boston. Like P&O, Cunard is only able to operate profitably because of the government mail contract it obtains

1841 Great Western Railway from London to Bristol opens. Created by Isambard Kingdom Brunel, it uses the 7-foot broad gauge rather than Stephenson's standard gauge of 4-foot, 8.5 inches

1843 Great Britain, 3,500 tons, a radical departure with its iron hull and screw propellor rather than paddle wheels. Its example is decisive in converting the Royal Navy to steam

1843 Shanghai is opened to Western trade after the end of the First Opium War. Hong Kong has recently been ceded to Britain and the East India Company's monopoly on the China trade ended. The way is open for the fast tea clippers, the first being the Oriental from New York, in 1849. These are the ultimate development of the cargo-carrying sailing ship with their streamlined hulls and huge quantity of sails, designed to get their cargoes of tea home as fast as possible to avoid deterioration. In 1851 the Australian Gold Rush comes as a further stimulus, and then the need to get Australian wool to England to meet fixed auction dates

1852 There are now 7,500 miles of railway in Britain and main routes between all regions are completed

1858 Great Eastern, 18,914 tons, is launched, powered by paddles, screw and sails and for many years the world's largest ship. Together with the Great Western and the Great Britain, it is the inspiration of Isambard Kingdom Brunel, whose Great Western Railway is to be taken into Cornwall via his Saltash Bridge across the river Tamar the following year

1866 The great race between the clippers Ariel, Taeping and Serica, all built by Steele of Greenock. All leave Foo-chow-foo on the same day and all get to London 99 days later, the same day that the Cutty Sark is launched. The Suez Canal opens three years later and marks the end of the clipper era.

1880 Steam tonnage finally equals sail tonnage in the British merchant marine

'As to those persons who speculate on making railways general throughout the kingdom, and superseding all the canals, all the wagons, mail and stage-coaches, post-chaises, and, in short, every other mode of conveyance by land and by water, we deem them and their visionary schemes unworthy of notice... The gross exaggerations of the powers of the locomotive steam-engine, or, to speak in plain English, the steam carriage, may delude for a time, but must end in the mortification of those concerned.'
– *The Quarterly Review*, 1825

THE SIXTH-FORM EXAMINATION PAPER IN MODERN HISTORY AT HARROW SCHOOL IN 1829

1. Who are the principal authorities for universal chronology?

2. Enumerate the various corrections which the solar year has undergone.

3. State the different modes of computing the year among the ancient Greeks, the Romans, the Jews, the Franks, the French, and the English.

4. Give an account of the Diocletian era, the mundane era of Constantinople, mundane era, modern Jews, Spanish era, era of Hegira, and Dionysian or Christian era.

5. Give the original site of the Vandals, Goths, Franks, Saxons, and Huns.

6. State the original sources from which we derive our knowledge of events from the reign of Nerva to that of Justinian.

7. Give an outline of the history of the Franks from their passage of the Rhine to the treaty of Verdun, with dates.

8. The conquests of the Visigoths and Vandals, with the ultimate fate of their monarchies, with dates.

9. When did the Romans abandon Britain? When and by whom was Christianity introduced into this country? What was the origin of the common law of England?

10. Draw a parallel between the characters of Alfred and Charlemagne.

The Schoolroom at Harrow

THE VICTORIAN AGE

HOSTILITIES DURING
THE 'LONG PEACE', 1815–1899

The years between the Battle of Waterloo in 1815 and the outbreak of the Second Boer War in 1899 have often been called the 'Long Peace'. In 1973 Byron Farwell demonstrated what a misnomer that is by listing nearly all the major and minor actions between 1837 and 1899 in his book *Queen Victoria's Little Wars*. To his list, printed below, there can be added the major campaigns between 1815 and 1837, to give the complete picture from the end of the Napoleonic Wars. If no country is given at the end of an entry, assume the location is the Indian Empire or its borders.

1816	Conclusion of the Gurkha War
	Bombardment of Algiers by Anglo-Dutch fleet
1817	Third Mahratta War
1818	Third Kandyan War in Sri Lanka
1824–26	First Burma War
1826	Capture of Bhurtpore
1830s–40s	Xosa Wars in South Africa
1837	Insurrection in Canara
1837–38	Mackenzie's rebellion in Ontario
	Second Goomsore campaign
1839	Operations in the Persian Gulf
	Kurnool campaign
	Capture of Aden
	Jodhpur campaign
1839–42	First Afghan War
	First Opium War in China
1840	Expedition into Kohistan
	Marri uprising in Sind
	Operations on the coast of Syria
1841	Expedition into Zurmatt
	Expedition against dacoits in Shahjehanpore district
1842	Expedition against Walleng hill tribes on the Arracan frontier, Burma
	Expedition against Shinwaris
	Pirara expedition, Guyana
	Insurrection in Shorapore district
	Bundlecund campaign
	Industrial disturbances at Leeds
	Military occupation of Natal
1842–43	Operations in the Saugor and Nerbudda territories
	Rebecca riots in Wales

	Sind campaign
	Gwalior campaign
	Pirates of Borneo chastised
	Disturbance in Malabar
1843–8	First Maori War, New Zealand
1844	Mutiny of two native regiments on Sind frontier
1844–5	Campaign in southern Mahratta country
	Campaign against hill tribes on northern frontier of Sind
1845	Expedition against Boers, South Africa
	Suppression of pirates in Borneo
	Naval action against Argentines on Parana River
1845–6	First Sikh War
1846	Aden besieged
1846–7	Kaffir War (War of the Ax), South Africa
1847	Capture of the Bogue forts, China
	Rebellion in Golcondah and Darcondah in the Golondah Zemindary
1847–8	Expedition to Goomsore
1848	Sherbo expedition
	White Cloud expedition against the Braves, Canada
	Expedition against King of Appolonia on Gold Coast, West Africa
	Rebellion in Ceylon
	Action at Boomplaats against disaffected Boers
1848–9	Second Sikh War
1849	Expedition against Baizai
1849–50	Expedition against Afridis
1850	Mutiny of 66th Native Infantry, India
	Expedition against Kohat Pass Afridis
1850–3	Kaffir War
1851	Expedition against Miranzai
	Occupation of Bahadoor Khail
	Bombardment of Lagos, Nigeria
	Siege of Dhasore
	Operations against Umarzai Waziris
1851–2	Two expeditions against Momands
	First Basuto War, actually two separate affairs, one in '51 and another in '52, in South Africa
1852	Expedition against Umarzai Waziris
	Expedition against Ranizais
	Expedition against Afridis
1852–3	Expedition to Black Mountains to punish Hasanzais
	Second Burma War
1853	Expedition against Kasranis
	Expedition against Hindustani Fanatics

	Expedition against Shiranis
	Expedition against Bori clan of Jowaki Afridis
1854	Expedition against Mohmands
	Battle of Muddy Flat
	Rebellion of Burmese in Bassein district
	Operations against Rohillas
	Relief of Christenborg on Gold Coast
	Riots of Chinese in Singapore
	Eureka Stockade incident, Australia
	Operations against rebels in Tondiman Rajah's country
1845–55	Malageah expeditions
	Crimean War
1855	Expedition against Aka Khel Afridis
	Expedition against Miranzai
	Expedition against Rubia Khel Orakzais
	Insurrection of Bedeers of Deodroog
	Storming of Sabbajee
1855–6	Insurrection of the Sonthals suppressed
1856	Expedition against Turis
	Fights with hill Kareems in Burma
1856–7	Persian War
1856–60	Arrow or Second Opium War in China
1857	Operations in Canton River, China
	Operations against Shans and Kareens of the Younzareen district, Martaban Province
	Expedition against Beydur Beluchis
	Expedition to the Bozdar hills
	Expedition against hill tribes in Rajahmundry district
	Expedition against villages on the Yusafzai border
	Island of Perim in the Strait of Bab-el-Mandeb (near Aden) occupied
1857–60	Indian Mutiny
1858	Expedition against Khudu Khels and Hindustani fanatics
	Expedition against the Crobboes
1858–59	Expedition against Singhbhum rebels
1859	Great Scarcies River expedition
	Bundlecund campaign
	Expedition against Kabul Khel Waziris
	Expedition against the Dounquah rebels
1859–62	The 'Blue Mutiny' in Bengal
1860	Expedition against Mahsud Waziris
1860–61	Baddiboo War on the Gambia, W. Africa
	Maori War
	Sikkim expedition
	Quiah War in Sierra Leone

1861	Storming and capture of Rohea
	Disturbances in Honduras
	Attack on Madoukia
	Expedition against Porto Novo, Dahomey, West Africa
	Bombardment and destruction of Massougha on Sierra Leone River
1862–3	Cossiah Rebellion
1863	Umbeyla campaign
	Action against Malay Pirates
1863–4	First Ashanti War
1863–6	Maori War
1864	Operations against shore batteries in Japan
	Bhutan expedition
	Expedition against the Mohmands
1865	Insurrection of freed slaves in Jamaica
	Bombardment of Cape Haitian in Haiti
1865–6	Expedition into interior of Arabia from Aden
1866	Fenian troubles in Ireland
1867	Fenian troubles in Ireland
	Expedition to Honduras
	Expedition to Little Andaman Island
1867–8	Abyssinian War
1868	Expedition against Bizoti Orakzais
	Hazara expedition against Black Mountain tribes
	Basuto War, Africa
1868–70	Maori War in New Zealand
1869	Expedition against Bizoti Orakzais
1869–70	Red River expedition in Canada
1870	Fenian raid from United States into Canada
1871–2	Lushai campaign
1872	Expedition against Dawaris
1873	Town of Omoa in Spanish Honduras bombarded
1873–4	Second Ashanti War
1874–5	Daffla expedition on North-West Frontier
1875	Naga Hills expedition
	Bombardment of villages on Congo River
	Rebellion in Griqualand, South Africa
1875–6	Rebellion of slavers against British imposed anti-slavery laws in Mombasa and Kilwa, East Africa
	Operations in Malay Peninsula
1877–8	Kaffir War
	Expedition against Jawaki Afridis
1878	Pirate strongholds in Borneo bombarded
	Gaika War in South Africa
	Expedition against Zakha Khel Afridis

1878–80	Second Afghan War
1879	Expedition against Zakha Khel Afridis
	Expedition against Suliman Khel Pawindahs and others
	Punitive expedition against Zaumukts
	Expedition against Mohmands
	Zulu War
	Expedition against Sekakuni
1879–80	Naga expedition
1880	Expedition against Batanis
	Expedition against Marris
	Expedition against Mohmands
	Expedition against Malikshahi Waziris
1880–1	The Gun War or Fifth Basuto War
	First Anglo-Boer War
1881	Expedition against Mahsud Waziris
1882	Arabi rebellion, Egypt
1883	Bikaneer expedition
1883–4	Akha expedition
1884	Rebellion of Metis in Western Canada
	Zhob Valley expedition
1884–5	Expedition to Bechuanaland, South Africa
	Gordon Relief expedition, Sudan
1885	Bhutan expedition
1885–7	Third Burma War
1885–98	Wars with Arab slave traders in Nyasa, Africa
1888	Black Mountain or Hazara expedition
1888–9	Sikkim expedition
1889	Tonhon expedition
	Expedition to Sierra Leone
1889–90	Chin Lushai campaign
1890	Malakand campaign
	Mashonaland expedition, Africa
	Vitu expedition
	Punitive expedition in Somaliland
1891	Manipur expedition
	Hunza and Nagar campaign
	Samana or second Miranzai expedition
	Hazara expedition
1891–92	Operations in Uganda
	Campaign in Gambia
1892	Isazai expedition
	Tambi expedition
	Chin Hills expedition
1893	British and French shoot at each other by mistake in Sierra Leone
	First Matabele War

	Expedition to Nyasaland
1893–4	Third Ashanti War
	Arbor Hills expedition
1894	Gambia expedition
	Disturbances in Nicaragua
	British expedition to Sierra Leone
	Expedition against Kabarega, King of Unyoro, in Uganda
1894–5	Punitive expedition to Waziristan
	Nikki expedition
1895	Chitral campaign
	Brass River expedition, Nigeria
1895–6	Second Matabele War
	Jameson Raid, South Africa
	Fourth Ashanti War
1896	Bombardment of Zanzibar
	Rebellion in Rhodesia
	Matabele uprising
1896–8	Reconquest of Sudan
1897	Operations in Bechuanaland
	Operation in Bara Valley
1897–8	Punitive expedition into Tochi Valley
	Tirah campaign
	Uganda mutiny
1897–1903	Conquest of Northern Nigeria (capture of Benin City in 1897)
1898	Riots in Crete, bombardment of Candia
1898–1902	Suppression of the Mad Mullah in Somaliland
1899	Campaign in Sierra Leone
	Bebejiya Expedition, North-East Frontier
1899–1902	Anglo-Boer War
1900	Boxer Rebellion
	Aden field force supported Haushabi fight off Humar tribe from Yemen
	Rebellion in Borneo
1900–1	Ashanti War

THE FREE-TRADE HAT

The ANTI-CORN LAW LEAGUE campaigned for the ending of the customs duties on imported corn imposed in 1815. It was formed in 1839, as recorded by this label, designed to be stuck inside the crown of a top hat. It could call on the support of labourers, anxious for cheaper bread for their families, and of their middle-class employers eager to avoid agitation for higher wages at a time of rising food prices. As JOHN BRIGHT, one of the League's leaders, said, it was 'a movement of the commercial and industrious classes against the lords and great proprietors of the soil'. Interest in the League actually declined somewhat after 1844 when this label was printed by Mr Marriott, an enterprising South London hatter trying to combine marketing of his products with a political message. But the League was unknowingly pushing against an open door because the Tory Prime Minister, SIR ROBERT PEEL, had already convinced himself that the duties would have to go. As early as 1841 he said, 'You might on moral and social grounds prefer cornfields to cotton factories, but our lot is cast, we cannot recede.' The outbreak of the IRISH POTATO FAMINE at the end of 1845 decided him to repeal the Corn Laws the following year. A further irony is that because of a worldwide shortage of grain, wheat was ten shillings a quarter more expensive by the late 1850s than it had been at the start of that decade. Then the outbreak of the American Civil War in 1861 further postponed the era of cheap food until the 1870s. A loaf which cost 1s 5d in 1873 cost 4 d in 1905.

The top and bottom segments of the label show British exports speeding on their way by rail and American exports going by sea. Those to right and left show British cotton goods and metalware being produced, American wheat being harvested, American pork being put into barrels, and bales and barrels of American cotton and tobacco awaiting shipment. The centre has scenes of a British family before and after the hoped-for repeal.

PUNCH'S VIEW OF SOCIETY IN 1841

That year the new humorous weekly *Punch* published a table of the different classes in London society. 'People who talk of the four per cents' would have liked to be taken for 'rentiers' living off the interest on their investments in government stocks, but were actually involved in grocery, in 'trade'. To 'confess the Cape' was perhaps to serve South African rather than French wine. A 'dry-salter' was a dealer in salted or dried meat and fish. A 'shay' was a chaise, a small carriage; the 'dog days' were from July 3 to August 11. The 'light porter in livery' was probably an employee of the 'concern' dressed up as a footman for the evening. 'White Conduit Gardens' was a place of entertainment in Islington where, by the 1820s, spectaculars and risqué shows were put on. 'Bluchers' were half-boots named after the Prussian commander, as opposed to the longer Wellington boots. 'Wans' were vans. The area around St Giles-in-the-Fields still had a series of grossly overcrowded semi-criminal slum rookeries at this time.

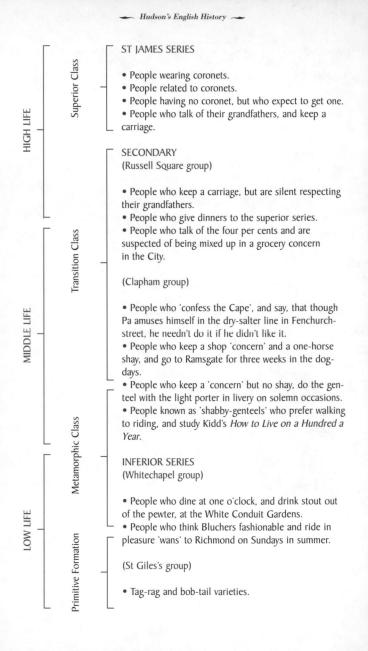

HIGH LIFE

Superior Class

ST JAMES SERIES

- People wearing coronets.
- People related to coronets.
- People having no coronet, but who expect to get one.
- People who talk of their grandfathers, and keep a carriage.

SECONDARY
(Russell Square group)

- People who keep a carriage, but are silent respecting their grandfathers.
- People who give dinners to the superior series.
- People who talk of the four per cents and are suspected of being mixed up in a grocery concern in the City.

MIDDLE LIFE

Transition Class

(Clapham group)

- People who 'confess the Cape', and say, that though Pa amuses himself in the dry-salter line in Fenchurch-street, he needn't do it if he didn't like it.
- People who keep a shop 'concern' and a one-horse shay, and go to Ramsgate for three weeks in the dog-days.
- People who keep a 'concern' but no shay, do the gen-teel with the light porter in livery on solemn occasions.
- People known as 'shabby-genteels' who prefer walking to riding, and study Kidd's *How to Live on a Hundred a Year*.

Metamorphic Class

INFERIOR SERIES
(Whitechapel group)

- People who dine at one o'clock, and drink stout out of the pewter, at the White Conduit Gardens.
- People who think Bluchers fashionable and ride in pleasure 'wans' to Richmond on Sundays in summer.

LOW LIFE

Primitive Formation

(St Giles's group)

- Tag-rag and bob-tail varieties.

MAJOR NEW PROFESSIONAL INSTITUTIONS IN THE 19TH CENTURY

Royal College of Surgeons .... chartered 1800
Apothecaries .... Act of Parliament 1815
Institution of Civil Engineers .... set up 1818, chartered 1828
The Law Society (solicitors) .... founded 1825, chartered 1837
Institute of British Architects .... founded 1835, chartered 1837
Pharmaceutical Society .... chartered 1844
Royal College of Veterinary Surgeons .... chartered 1847
Institution of Mechanical Engineers .... chartered 1847
Society of Accountants in Edinburgh .... chartered 1854
Institute of Accountants and Actuaries
in Glasgow .... chartered 1855
Society of Accountants in Aberdeen .... chartered 1867
Institution of Electrical Engineers .... chartered 1871
Institute of Chartered Accountants, London .... chartered 1880
Surveyors' Institution .... chartered 1881
Institute of Chemistry .... chartered 1884
Institute of Patent Agents .... chartered 1891
Library Association .... chartered 1898
Institute of Secretaries .... chartered 1902

THE GREAT EXHIBITION OF 1851

1848 The idea emerges from among council members of the Royal Society of Arts, originally founded in the mid-18th century 'for the encouragement of arts, manufactures and commerce'.

1849 It picks up momentum once Prince Albert gives his support, and it is agreed that it should be an international show funded by subscriptions, not by Parliament.

1850 The plans for the exhibition building in Hyde Park meet with hostility. A low structure, it requires 19 million bricks, though surmounted by a dome of iron and glass designed by I. K. Brunel. Joseph Paxton, who built the 'Great Stove', a greenhouse covering an acre, in 1840 for his employer the Duke of

Devonshire, draws up plans for an all-glass-and-iron building in nine days, and they are swiftly accepted. Work begins in September.

1851 January The building itself, christened the Crystal Palace by *Punch* magazine, is completed, thanks to the use of prefabricated components and 76 'glazing wagons' whose wheels run along the gutters and on which the workmen sit with their tools and materials. The transept, with its distinctive curved roof, has been added to the original design so that three large elm trees can be accommodated, in response to a public outcry, even though a thousand trees have recently been felled in the Park without protest. The building's south front stretches for exactly 1851 feet from opposite Knightsbridge Barracks in the east, nearly reaching the road separating Hyde Park from Kensington Gardens in the west.

'SPARROWHAWKS, MA'AM' The story that this was the Duke of Wellington's reply to Queen Victoria, when she asked how the problem of birds that had got into the building should be solved, is sadly untrue.

1851 May The Exhibition is opened by Queen Victoria, and she visits it regularly thereafter. A Chinese mandarin is among the dignitaries at the opening, but he turns out to be merely the captain of a junk moored in the Thames as a tourist attraction. Walter Bagehot, a journalist in a gallery close to the Queen, cannot hear a word of the opening ceremony and dismisses the whole thing as 'a great fair under a cucumber frame'. The British section occupying half the total area is well-nigh complete, but many foreign exhibits are still to be installed.

CATERING, in the hands of the Schweppes mineral water company, is much criticised, but 934,691 Bath buns, 33 tons of ham and 1,092,337 bottles of Schweppes soda water, lemonade and ginger beer are consumed, among much other food and drink

SIX MILLION TICKETS are sold, which means about a quarter of the British population see the Exhibition. Entry is a shilling, except on Fridays when it's two shillings and sixpence and Saturdays when it's five shillings (closed on Sundays). On shilling days attendances are regularly above 50,000; the largest attendance on one day is 109,915. Over 827,000 pay a penny to use the public conveniences (urinals are free). All flush.

EXHIBITS Some machinery can work because of steam engines located just outside the building. The most popular items from America are McCormick's reaping machine and Colt's revolver. I.K. Brunel's demand that all electrical exhibits be banned since they are nothing better than toys is ignored. As well as more conventional exhibits, there are:

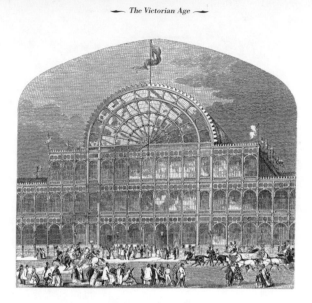

The Koh-i-Noor diamond, recently taken as booty from the Sikh royal family
De la Rue's patent envelope machine, producing 60 a minute
A knife with 1851 blades
A buttonless shirt for bachelors who can't sew
Furniture made of coal
A mechanism for tipping one out of bed in the morning
Hats made of cork
A straw chandelier

1851 October The Exhibition closes, leaving a surplus of £186,000, which goes towards the purchase of 70 acres, on which the Victoria & Albert, the Science and the Natural History Museums, Imperial College, the Royal College of Music, the Royal Geographical Society and the Albert Hall are later built. It has also been the making of Charles Harrod's grocery store in Knightsbridge.

1854 The Crystal Palace re-opens after re-erection at Sydenham in South London. It has been enlarged so that it has half as much floor space again, and is crammed with paintings, educational exhibits, statues, architectural models, tropical trees and a concert hall. Its grounds are dotted with lifesize models of dinosaurs.

1936 The Crystal Palace burns down.

THE RELIGIOUS CENSUS OF 1851

On Mid-Lent or Mothering Sunday, the 30th of March that year, for the first and last time all those attending places of worship in England and Wales in the morning, afternoon or evening were counted, and this produced the following figures:

	Persons at Church	Percentage of total population
Church of England	2,971,258	17
Nonconformist	3,110,782	17
Roman Catholic	249,389	1
Sectarian	24,793	(.1)
TOTAL	6,356,222	35

(Out of a total population of about 18 million)

These figures came as a considerable jolt, showing as they did that 65 per cent of the population were 'habitual neglecters of the public ordnances of religion', and that Nonconformist church and chapel-goers outnumbered those attending Church of England services. Further analysis demonstrated that organised religion – Anglicanism in particular – had failed lamentably to spread the Word among the new town-dwelling masses.

Putting to one side the Roman Catholics, particularly strong in Lancashire, and the High, Broad and Low persuasions within the Church of England, it is the Nonconformists who present the most confusing picture, as the diagram indicates. However, it is somewhat simplified when it is remembered that half of all Nonconformists were Methodists of some kind, a quarter were Congregationalists and 20 per cent were Baptists. Nonconformity was weak in London, dominant in Wales and strong in the urban industrial towns, with Wesleyan Methodism predominating. That type was also strong in Cornwall, as was Primitive Methodism in Lincolnshire, the East Riding of Yorkshire and Norfolk, while there were many Particular Baptists in Monmouthshire, Bedfordshire and Huntingdonshire.

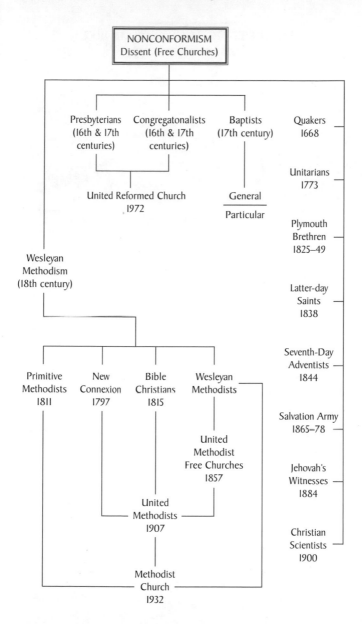

NONCONFORMISM
Dissent (Free Churches)

Presbyterians (16th & 17th centuries)

Congregationalists (16th & 17th centuries)

Baptists (17th century)

Quakers 1668

United Reformed Church 1972

General
Particular

Unitarians 1773

Plymouth Brethren 1825–49

Wesleyan Methodism (18th century)

Latter-day Saints 1838

Seventh-Day Adventists 1844

Primitive Methodists 1811

New Connexion 1797

Bible Christians 1815

Wesleyan Methodists

Salvation Army 1865–78

United Methodist Free Churches 1857

Jehovah's Witnesses 1884

United Methodists 1907

Christian Scientists 1900

Methodist Church 1932

MRS BEETON'S MENUS FOR A WEEK OF PLAIN FAMILY DINNERS, 1861

SUNDAY
Clear Gravy Soup. Roast Haunch of Mutton. Sea Kale. Potatoes. Rhubarb Tart. Custard in Glasses.

MONDAY
Crimped Skate and Caper Sauce. Boiled Knuckle of Veal and Rice. Cold Mutton. Stewed Rhubarb and Baked Custard Pudding.

TUESDAY
Vegetable Soup. Toad in the Hole, made from the remains of cold mutton. Stewed Rhubarb and Baked Plum Pudding.

WEDNESDAY
Fried Soles. Dutch Sauce. Boiled Beef, carrots, suet dumplings. Lemon Pudding.

THURSDAY
Pea Soup made from liquor that beef was boiled in. Cold Beef. Mashed Potatoes. Mutton Cutlets and Tomato Sauce. Macaroni.

FRIDAY
Bubble and Squeak, made with remains of cold beef. Roast Shoulder of Veal, stuffed, and spinach and potatoes. Boiled Batter Pudding and Sweet Sauce.

SATURDAY
Stewed Veal and Vegetables, made from remains of the shoulder. Broiled rumpsteaks and oyster sauce. Yeast Dumplings.

GREAT VICTORIAN LANDOWNERS

In 1883 John Bateman published *The Great Landowners of Great Britain and Ireland*. This showed that 400 peers and peeresses owned between them about 5.7 million acres; that there were 1,288 commoners with 3,000 acres or more, or £3,000 rental, owning a total of 8.5 million acres; and that there were 2,529 commoners with between 1,000 and 3,000 acres, or up to £3,000 rental, owning 4.3 million acres. These three acreages added together amounted to 56.3 per cent of the cultivated acreage in Great Britain and Ireland. He also listed landowners with a gross annual income of more than £100,000, but made various errors such as omitting London property. A revised list of those with such incomes was drawn up by W. D. Rubinstein in his book *Men of Property* in 1981:

LANDOWNER	INCOME (£)
Duke of Westminster	c. 290,000–325,000
Duke of Buccleuch	232,000
Duke of Bedford	225,000–250,000
Duke of Devonshire	181,000
Duke of Northumberland	176,000
Earl of Derby	163,000
Marquess of Bute	153,000
Duke of Sutherland	142,000
Duke of Hamilton	141,000
Earl Fitzwilliam	139,000
Earl of Dudley	123,000
Earl of Ancaster	121,000
Marquess of Anglesey	111,000
Marquess of Londonderry	110,000
Duke of Portland	108,000
Marquess of Hertford	104,000
Viscount Portman	c. 100,000

Bateman also gave what he considered a fair specimen of what a landed income of £5,000 a year, from a notional 3,500 acres, 'meant when analysed'. He called his typical squire JOHN STEADYMAN OF WEARYWORK HALL, CIDERSHIRE, and showed that after deductions and expenses he was left 'the magnificent annual sum of £1,032 to live upon': (See over)

Born 1825, succeeded 1860, married 1851	ACRES	VALUE (£)
	3,500	5,000

Deduct for value in the rate-books put upon mansion, grounds, fishponds, etc. £220
Deduct also the value put upon cottages lived in rent-free by old workmen and pensioners of the late Mr Steadyman £30 250

Leaving a clear rent roll of 4,750

NOW DEDUCT AS UNDER:

• His late father's two maiden sisters, Jane and Esther Steadyman, who each have a rent charge of £180 per annum. (NB Both these old ladies seem immortal.) 360
• His mother, Lady Louisa Steadyman, a rent charge of 700
• His sisters, Louisa, Marian and Eva (all plain) each £150 450
• His brother, Wildbore Steadyman, who was paid off and emigrated but almost annually comes down on the good-natured head of the family for say 50
• Mortgage on Sloppyside Farm and Hungry Hill (started when his father contested the county as parliamentary candidate), interest 650
• Do. on Wearywork End (started when his one pretty sister married Sir Shortt Shortt, Bart. and was paid off), interest 150
• His estate agent, Mr Harrable, salary 150
• Keep of a horse for do. £35; house for do. £45 80
• Average of lawyer's bill (settlements, conveyances, etc.) 60
• Average cost of farm repairs, etc 350
• Draining tiles furnished gratis to the tenants 40
• Repairs to the family mansion 70
• Voluntary church rate, school at Wearywork, do. at Wearywork End, pensions, and purely local charities 175
(NB If Mr S. is a Roman Catholic, which I do not think he is, a private chaplain, chapel, school etc. would increase this to at least £225.)
• Subscription to county (Liberal or Tory) registration fund 10
• Do. to the Cidershire Foxhounds (£25) and
    Boggymore Harriers (£5) 30
• Do. to the Diocesan –? (everything now-a-days is Diocesan, we shall soon be taking pills from the Diocesan dispensaries) 25
• Other county subscriptions – hospitals, flower shows, races, etc. 35
• Returned 15% of rents in 'hard times' averaging perhaps one year in five (would that we could say so now, 1882) 150

- Loss on occasional bankrupt tenants
(Mr Harrable dislikes distraint), average 30
- Arrears of rent, say annually £300, loss of interest thereon at 5% 15
- Income-tax at 4*d* in the pound on rents paid and unpaid 83
- Insurance on all buildings 55

TOTAL .... £ 3,718

LARGEST BRITISH FORTUNES, 1809–1914

These are listed in order of date of death and the minimum amount is two million pounds. The Duke of Sutherland, Marquis of Bute and Earl Fitzwilliam also feature on the list of Great Victorian Landowners.

NAME, OCCUPATION, VENUE	VALUATION (£ THOUSANDS)
1. George, first Duke of Sutherland (1758-1833), landowner	'Upper Value' *
2. Nathan M. Rothschild (1777–1836), merchant banker in London	'Upper Value' **
3. James Morrison (1789–1857), warehouseman and merchant banker in London	c.4,000-6,000 ***
4. Sir Isaac L. Goldsmid, 1st Bt (1778–1859), bullion broker and merchant banker in London	c. 2,000#
5. William Baird (1796–1864), ironmaster in Lanarkshire, etc.	2,000
6. Richard Thornton (1776–1865), insurance broker and Baltic merchant in London	2,800
7. William Crawshay (1788–1867), ironmaster in South Wales	2,000
8. Thomas Brassey (1805–1870), railway contractor	3,200
9. Giles Loder (1786–1871), Russia merchant in London	2,900
10. Baron Mayer A. de Rothschild (1818–1874), merchant banker in London	2,100
11. Lionel N. de Rothschild (1808–1874), merchant banker in London	2,700
12. Samuel J.Loyd, first Baron Overstone (1796–1883), banker in London	2,119##
13. Herman, Baron de Stern (1815–1887), merchant banker in London	3,545
14. Hugh McCalmont (1809–1887), stockbroker and foreign merchant in London	3,122

37.	William H. Wills, first Baron Winterstoke (1830–1911), tobacco manufacturer in Bristol	2,548
38.	Peter Coats (1842–1913), sewing-thread manufacturer in Paisley	2,562
39.	Sir James Coats, 1st Bt (1834–1913), sewing-thread manufacturer in Paisley	2,548
40.	William Wier (1826–1913), ironmaster and colliery owner in Lanarkshire, etc.	2,220

* The precise value of his personalty, including the Bridgewater property that he inherited, is not known, but in 1883 the two heirs to his landed wealth, the Duke of Sutherland and the Earl of Ellesmere, were in receipt of a gross annual income of £213,000.

** Rothschild's fortune was estimated by contemporaries at up to £5 million.

*** This estimate was given by contemporary writers and in obituaries.

Estimated at this figure in the *Illustrated London News* of 11 June 1859.

Overstone also owned land costing over £1,500,000 to purchase.

+ Began life as a traveller in pen and watch materials, was a money-lender to the wealthy at Cork Street in Mayfair.

++ McCalmont inherited the bulk of the fortune of his great-uncle Hugh McCalmont (d. 1887), which had been left to gather interest for seven years after his death.

BELOW STAIRS

Around 1900 the indoors staff at Longleat, home of the Marquess of Bath, was still very substantial, even if only roughly half the size of Knole's in the reign of James I (p. 68). It consisted of:

House Steward
Butler
Under Butler
Groom of the Chambers
Valet
Three Footmen
Steward's Room Footman
Two Oddmen
Two Pantry boys
Lamp Boy

Housekeeper
Two Lady's Maids
Nurse
Nursery Maid
Eight Housemaids
Two Sewing Maids
Two Still Room Maids
Six Laundry Maids

Chef
Two Kitchen Maids
Vegetable Maid
Scullery Maid
Daily Woman

The Butler was in charge of the dining room and the cellars; the Groom of the Chambers looked after the reception rooms and the needs of visitors; the Third Footman was attached to the nursery. The Still Room was where rose water was distilled, pot pourri was made, fruit was preserved, jam was made, orange and lemon peel was candied, morello cherries were bottled in brandy and lavender was dried.

At lunch in the servants' hall, once the first course was finished, the joint which had been its centrepiece was carried out with some ceremony followed by a procession of the House Steward, Housekeeper, Butler, Cook, Lady's Maids, Valets and the Groom of the Chambers. This party retired to the Steward's Room to eat the rest of their lunch, while Housemaids and Sewing Maids took plates of pudding to their own sitting rooms.

The kitchen staff did not have to attend morning prayers in the chapel so was able to cook breakfast. There was a pond in the middle of the kitchen courtyard where trout and pike were kept alive after being caught so that any muddy taint to their flesh was removed. Three sheep a week were killed to keep the kitchen supplied with lamb and mutton: a Westmorland, a Southdown and a Brittany (the latter for small cutlets). Pots and pans were scoured with a mix of soft soap, ale and silver sand.

As well as the indoor staff there were 14 in the stables and then the gardeners, woodmen and gamekeepers. Among the 14 were a Steel Boy who polished bits and harness and a 'Tiger', a small youth whose job it was to sit on the box next to the coachman, ramrod straight with his arms folded. His other duty was to lead the children's ponies. There were dances twice a week in the servants' hall to which these outside staff also came.

The place taken by visiting servants within this hierarchy depended on the rank of their masters or mistresses. For instance, a royal maid would be escorted by the House Steward.

THE PROGRESS OF CIVILISATION IN 19TH-CENTURY BRITAIN

In 1851 the *Economist* published a series of articles comparing life in that year with life in 1801, commenting among much else that the sight of a drunken gentleman was now 'one of the rarest', whereas in 1801, 'many got drunk every day.' Its findings in relation to the cost of living and improvements in communications are set out below.

	1801	1851
Meat per stone (6.4 kg)	5s 8d	3s 4d
Bread per loaf	1s 10d	6d
Tea per pound	5s	3s 4d
Coffee per pound	2s	1s
Sugar per pound	8d	4d
Cotton cloth per yard	1s	3d

	1801	1851
Voyage to America	eight weeks	ten days
Fastest journeys on land	10 mph	63 mph
Letter, London–Edinburgh	seven days	one day
	cost 13½d	cost 1d
Urgent message	man on horseback	telegraph

In June 1887, after attending the service of thanksgiving at Westminster Abbey for the Golden Jubilee of Queen Victoria, the distinguished scientist Sir Lyon Playfair wrote to the Queen's private secretary, Sir Henry Ponsonby:

'On coming back from the Abbey, impressed deeply with the ceremony, I tried to form an index of the progress of civilisation during the Queen's reign. The result may interest you. The price of rags as indicating the demand for paper has always appeared to me the best index of progress and the following facts are striking:

'In 1837 each head of the population consumed 1.25lb of paper; in 1887 no lessthan 12lbs. Measured by this index England is now at the head of all nations in 1887.

England	12lbs of paper per head
United States	10lbs of paper per head
Germany	9lbs of paper per head
France	8lbs of paper per head
Italy	4lbs of paper per head

'In 1837 each person of the population spent 1s 11d on books and newspapers annually: in 1887 this had increased to 9s.

'In 1837 each person sent nine letters through the post: in 1887 this had increased to thirty-eight. An index of this kind is encouraging.

'Another index of well doing is the consumption of soap, because "Cleanliness is next to Godliness". This however has not increased so much as I could have wished:

1837	7.75lbs per head of soap
1887	10lbs per head of soap

Still a child born today has three years more of life than if born in 1837.'

SOURCES &
ACKNOWLEDGEMENTS

SOURCES AND ACKNOWLEDGEMENTS

Huntsmen and Hounds from the Constitutio Domus Regis compiled for King Stephen in W O Hassall, How They Lived, 1962.

Monks, Friars and Canons David Knowles, The Religious Orders in England, vol I, 1948; David Knowles and R Neville Hadcock, Medieval Religious Houses in England and Wales, 1953; R W Southern, Western Society and the Church in the Middle Ages, 1970.

Siege Glossary Philip Warner, Sieges of the Middle Ages, 1968.

Places of Pilgrimage E Duffy, The Stripping of the Altars, 1992; R C Finucane, Miracles and Pilgrims, 1995.

Longbow and Crossbow Jim Bradbury, The Medieval Archer, 1985; Robert Hardy, The Long Bow, 1992.

Plague and Disease William H McNeill, Plagues and Peoples, 1977; Philip Ziegler, The Black Death, 1982; Hans Zinsser, Rats, Lice and History, 1963.

Exchequer, Tallies M T Clanchy, England and its Rulers, 1066–1272, 1983, and M T Clanchy, From Memory to Written Word, 1979.

Pillory from the Liber Albus compiled by John Carpenter and Dick Whittington in W O Hassall, How They Lived, 1962.

Crafts in London W O Hassall, op. cit.; Ben Weinreb and Christopher Hibbert, The London Encyclopaedia, 1983.

Wool Trade Eileen Power, Medieval People, 1937.

Badges J P Brooke-Little, Boutell's Heraldry, 1983.

Falconry from The Boke of St Albans, 15th century. Phillip Glasier, Falconry and Hawking, 1978

Tudor Victims C R N Routh, Who's Who in Tudor Britain, 1990; Alison Weir, Britain's Royal Families, 2002.

Tudor Court David Loades, 'The Tudor Court', Historical Association booklet, 1989.

London Street Nuisances John Stow, Survey of London, 1598, 1603.

Opening of Parliament, 1563 J R Tanner, Tudor Constitutional Documents 1485–1603, 1930.

Border Clans George Macdonald Fraser, The Steel Bonnets, 1971. Map reproduced with permission of Curtis Brown Group Ltd, London on behalf of © George Macdonald Fraser 1971, © William Bromage 1971.

Armada William James, Naval History of Great Britain, 1837; J K Laughton, State Papers Relating to the Defeat of the Spanish Armada, 2 vols, 1894; Garrett Mattingley, The Defeat of the Spanish Armada, 1959.

Monopolies R H Tawney and Eileen Power eds, Tudor Economic Documents, vol II, 1924.

Beggars Frank Ayedelotte, Elizabethan Rogues and Vagabonds, 1913.

Inns of Court Roger Hudson, Fleet Street, Holborn and the Inns of Court, 1995.

Noble Household V Sackville-West, Knole and the Sackvilles, 1922.

Ranks Keith Wrightson, English Society 1580–1680, 1982.

Banquets V Sackville-West, Knole and the Sackvilles, 1922.

London Deaths J R McCulloch, A Statistical Account of the British Empire, vol II, 2nd edition, 1839.

Charles II's Bastards Alison Weir, Britain's Royal Families, 2002.

Town Growth Angus McInnes, 'The English Town 1660–1760', Historical Association booklet, 1980; Geoffrey Best, Mid-Victorian Britain, 1971.

Highwaymen D B Horn and Mary Ransome eds, English Historical Documents 1714–83, vol VII, 1957.

Oxford Jan Morris, Oxford Book of Oxford, 1978.

Bath William Connor Sydney, England and the English in the Eighteenth Century, vol II, 1891.

Living in London Asa Briggs, How They Lived 1700–1815, 1969.

Highland Clans Kenneth MacLeay, Delia Millar, Amelia Murray MacGregor, The Highlanders of Scotland, 1986; John Prebble, Culloden, 1961.

Waterways Map from John Rule, The Vital Century 1714–1815, Longman (Viking Penguin), 1992.

Gin: Jessica Warner, Craze: Gin and Debauchery in an Age of Reason, 2003.

Workhouse A Aspinall and E Anthony Smith eds, English Historical Documents 1783–1832, vol VIII, 1959.

Tax J R McCulloch, A Statistical Account of the British Empire, vol II, 2nd edition, 1839.

Industrial Revolution: Peter Burke ed, The New Cambridge Modern History, Companion vol XIII, Ch 3, Industry, by William N Parker, 1979. By permission of Cambridge University Press.

Spinners' Fines Asa Briggs, How They Lived 1700–1815, 1969.

Cotton and Wool C R Fay, Life and Labour in the Nineteenth Century, 1920.

Living in Leeds B W Clapp, Documents in English Economic History: Since 1760, 1976.

Population Asa Briggs, How They Lived 1700–1815, 1969; Geoffrey Best, Mid-Victorian Britain, 1971.

Elections William Connor Sydney, England and the English in the Eighteenth Century, vol II, 1891; Michael Brock, The Great Reform Act, 1973. Anthony Henley's letter reproduced by kind permission of Lord Henley.

Nelson's Navy Classification of ships derived from Nicholas Blake and Richard Lawrence, The Illustrated Companion to Nelson's Navy, 1999, by kind permission of Chatham Publishing; William James, Naval History of Great Britain, 1837.

Deaths in the Peninsula J R McCulloch, A Statistical Account of the British Empire, vol II, 2nd edition, 1839.

Continental Subsidies A Aspinall and E Anthony Smith eds, English Historical Documents 1783–1832, vol VIII, 1959.

French Defeats Derived, with kind permission, from a list compiled by Adrian Sykes.

Purchase of Commissions A Aspinall and E Anthony Smith eds, op. cit.

Death Sentence J R McCulloch, op. cit.

Sail and Steam Adrian Vaughan, Railwaymen, Politics and Money, 1997; Ronald Hope, A New History of British Shipping, 1990.

History Exam A Aspinall and E Anthony Smith eds, op. cit.

Hostilities 1815–99 Byron Farwell, Queen Victoria's Little Wars, Allen Lane (Viking Penguin), 1973.

Professions W J Reader, Professional Men, 1966.

Religion in 1851 Geoffrey Best, Mid-Victorian Britain, 1971; Francois Bedarida, A Social History of England 1851–1990, Routledge, 1991.

Great Landowners John Bateman, The Great Landowners of Great Britain and Ireland, 1883; W D Rubinstein, Men of Property, Croom Helm, 1981. By kind permission of Professor Rubenstein.

Largest Fortunes W D Rubinstein, Elites and the Wealthy in Modern British History, Harvester Press, 1987. By kind permission of Professor Rubenstein.

Below Stairs The Marchioness of Bath, Before the Sunset Fades, 1951.

Progress Arthur Ponsonby, Henry Ponsonby, 1942.